Dad Mode: On

The Book for New and Expecting Fathers, Navigating First-Time Fatherhood and Best Tips

CW01080569

Marshall O'Neal

Introduction

Welcome, future dads! Are you ready for the most exhilarating and inspiring journey of your life? If you are holding this book, it means you are interested in being the best father for your child, and I am here to help you every step of the way.

This book is your friendly advisor and steadfast companion on the journey to fatherhood. I have gathered advice, scientific facts, real stories, and the wisdom of fathers who have been through it before you, to make your path a little easier and much more enjoyable.

Preparing for fatherhood may seem complicated and daunting, but fear not! Together, we will navigate how to support your partner, how to prepare for the baby's arrival, how to overcome obstacles, and most importantly, how to enjoy every moment of this amazing time.

You will learn how to support your pregnant partner, how to find balance in emotional storms (yes, men have emotional ups and downs too!), and how to prepare for unexpected surprises in the middle of the night. And who knows, maybe you will even become a master at choosing baby products and setting up the nursery without stress and hassle!

Together, we will laugh at absurdities, learn from mistakes, and find joy in the little things. Because fatherhood is not just a duty and responsibility, it is an adventure, full of laughter, love, and incredible discoveries.

So, relax, open your mind and heart, and join me on this wonderful journey. Many amazing moments and unforgettable memories await you. Welcome to the fathers' club, where every day is a new adventure!

Table of Contents

CHAPTER 1:

The News Just Dropped, Now What?

1.1 Shock and Awe: Navigating That 'Oh My Gosh, I'm Going to Be a Dad' Moment

Hey there, soon-to-be-dad! So, you've just heard the news. Maybe it was a text with a picture of a pregnancy test or a more dramatic revelation, complete with a heartfelt talk. Whatever the case, welcome to the club! Shocked? Maybe a bit awestruck? Yeah, me too when it was my turn. But listen, it's completely normal.

First things first, take a deep breath. No, seriously, do it. You just got hit with a life-changer, and those lungs need all the oxygen they can get right now. Done? Alright, let's move on.

It's easy to start thinking about, well, everything—diapers, college funds, what kind of dad you'll be—but hold your horses. You've got time. Sure, many changes are coming, but they aren't happening overnight. You're just at the starting line of this marathon, not midway through.

Let's talk reaction. How did you react when you heard the news? Hopefully, it was supportive—even if you were doing cartwheels or hyperventilating inside. But let's be real: no one hands you an instruction manual for moments like these. So, if your reaction wasn't out of a storybook, don't sweat it. You'll have plenty of opportunities to be the rockstar dad-to-be.

Your partner is also likely going through her whirlwind of emotions. So, buddy system—stick together. She needs to know you're on board, even if you're internally still at the train station trying to buy a ticket. My advice? Keep the lines of communication open from the get-go. You're in this as a team, not as solo artists trying to perform your renditions of "Parenting for Dummies."

If you're a planner like me, you might be tempted to start reading, Googling, and maybe even building a crib from scratch—easy, tiger. You'll get to all that. But for now, let the news settle in. You don't have to have it all figured out today or even tomorrow. Just remember, shock fades, awe turns into love, and before you know it, you'll be holding a little package that somehow manages to pee, poop, and look adorable simultaneously.

So, shake off that deer-in-the-headlights look and get ready for a wild, rewarding ride best described as 'organized chaos.' You've got this. And if you ever doubt it, well, that's what this book is for. Onward, soldier!

1.2 Do the Math: Your New Budget Reality

So, now that the initial shock has worn off—or at least you're getting used to the idea—let's talk dollars and cents. Or should I say diapers and baby wipes? Either way, things are about to get a whole lot more expensive. But don't start freaking out. We're not headed for financial ruin; we're just gearing up for a bit of lifestyle renovation.

First up, you'll need a budget. Ah, the B-word. If you've been winging it up till now, those freewheeling days are about to meet the Responsible You. Time to sit down and hash out what's coming in and going out. Income, expenses, all that jazz. And don't you dare try to do it all in your head. Use a spreadsheet, old-school pen and paper, or even one of those budgeting apps. Just ensure you actually do it.

Think beyond the immediate, like diapers and formula. We're talking the long game here—new furniture, possible medical expenses, heck, even saving for their education (yeah, it's never too early for that). Factor it all in so you're not blindsided later.

Now, I get it. The numbers might start looking overwhelming, like some doomsday stock market crash. But here's the thing: there are always ways to trim the fat. Maybe you cut back on eating out, or perhaps those weekly golf sessions turn into monthly ones. The point is that some of your luxuries might need to be sidelined for life's latest arrival.

If you haven't already, this is also the time to have the "Who's working, who's staying home?" conversation with your partner. Are you both going back to work? Is one of you cutting back hours or quitting entirely? There are no right or wrong answers here, just the ones that make sense for your family.

It's okay to feel the pinch. Heck, who wouldn't? You're making room for another human in your life, and last I checked, they don't give those away for free at the hospital. But while you're grappling with the numbers, remember that not everything has a price tag. Sure, there's a financial cost, but the return on investment in love and joy is off the charts.

Takeaways? Do the math, adjust the sails, and keep a cool head. Life's about to get richer in so many more ways than one. And when you're elbow-deep in baby wipes and midnight feedings, trust me, the last thing you'll be thinking about is your wallet.

1.3 The Big Announcement: Telling Friends and Family

Alright, Captain Courageous, ready to spread the word? I can already see you daydreaming about that epic reveal—maybe you're imagining fireworks, skywriting, or even a full-blown Broadway musical number. But let's pump the brakes a sec and chat about when and how to tell people that a mini-you is en route.

First, you and your partner should be on the same page about timing. Some folks like to shout it from the rooftops as soon as they find out, while others prefer to wait until the first trimester is safely in the rearview mirror. Each approach has its pros and cons, so talk it over. You don't want to send out the bat signal before you both agree it's time.

Got the green light? Fantastic. Now, who gets to know first? I'd recommend starting with the VIPs—parents, siblings, closest friends. You know, the people who'll be genuinely thrilled and might actually offer to help with stuff like baby showers or hand-me-downs. How you tell them is up to you. In-person is ideal, but if that's impossible, a heartfelt phone call or video chat works too. No text breakers here, please—this is big news!

Alright, you've covered your inner circle. What's next? Time for the social media avalanche? Hold on there, hashtag hero. Before you go posting ultrasound pics or baby shoes, consider this: once the news is out there, it's out there. Are you and your partner ready for the onslaught of attention, advice, and possibly even judgment that might come your way? Think it through.

There's no one-size-fits-all strategy here. Some go for the big Facebook or Instagram reveal with balloons and clever captions. Others prefer a subtler, slow roll-out—gradually letting people in on the news, one casual conversation at a time. Choose the route that feels right for you.

And remember, not every reaction will be a home run. Aunt Gertrude might express concern over your readiness, or your gym buddy might worry about the end of your Spartan Race days. That's okay. Their reactions are theirs to own, not yours. Focus on the joy coming your way and the fun of sharing it.

So there you go, sport. Whether you go full-on Beyoncé-reveal-style or keep it low-key, the most important thing is to share the news in a way that feels authentic to you and your partner. After all, this is your first act as co-directors in this lifetime adventure. Make it count.

1.4 Morning Sickness Support: It's Not Just Her Problem

Feeling queasy yet? No, not you—I mean, are you helping your partner through the ups and downs of morning sickness? Trust me; as much as you might want to delegate this to the "pregnancy symptoms only she can experience" bucket, you're involved, too. Your role in this might not be biologically driven, but it's as critical as any job you've ever had. Trust me; you're in this as much as she is—just without the vomiting.

Morning sickness usually hits in the first trimester. But let's get one thing straight: the term "morning sickness" is a big fat misnomer. For some, it's "morning, noon, and night sickness." So, be prepared for anything.

First tip? Keep a sickness survival kit handy. Fill a bag with crackers, water, gum, and maybe some anti-nausea wristbands. Store it in places that make sense—like the car or near the bed. Believe me, nothing says, "I'm your hero," like handing your nauseated partner a cracker at just the right moment.

Now, let's talk about scents. Oh, man, you wouldn't believe how a pregnancy can turn a woman's nose into a CIA-level detector of smells. Your cologne, that leftover pizza in the fridge, even the neighbor's barbeque, anything can trigger a gag reflex. My advice? Play it safe and avoid strong smells when possible. You may need to give up your famous chili cook-off dreams for a few months, but it's a small price to pay for domestic harmony.

This is also a good time to be a good listener. If she says, "I can't stand the smell of coffee," for the love of all that's holy, don't brew a pot in the house.

The point is morning sickness isn't a solo sport; it's a team challenge. And while you're not the one hugging the porcelain throne, your support role is crucial. You can't take away the nausea, but you can make it a tad more bearable.

Hang in there, mate. This too shall pass, and then you'll be onto the next adventure of impending fatherhood. Ready to move on?

1.5 Early Doctor Visits: What You Should Know

Alright, ace, back in the saddle? Excellent. It's time to talk about those first trips to the doc—because, guess what? You're part of that package deal. Yes, the early doctor visits are crucial, and your presence is appreciated and pretty darn important. If you thought your only role at the OB/GYN's office was to hold a purse and leaf through outdated magazines in the waiting room, think again.

First things first: scheduling. You may think you're busy, but let me tell you, pregnancy busy is a whole different league. There are appointments to book, scans to schedule, and tests to be taken. Offer to take on some of that planning load. Create a shared calendar, set reminders, and do whatever it takes to help keep things organized.

When you walk into that doctor's office, you will be bombarded with information. I'm talking medical history, screenings, ultrasound schedules—the works. Your job? Listen. Take notes if you have to (yes, real notes, with a pen and everything). Being engaged shows your partner that you're fully on board this baby train, not just a passenger along for the ride.

Ultrasound day can be especially nerve-wracking but also thrilling. Trust me, seeing that tiny bean for the first time is a moment you don't want to miss. Be there to hold her hand because, let's face it, even the coolest cucumbers get a little jittery when it's time for that first glimpse.

Oh, and here's a pro tip: if the doc asks if you'd like to know the sex of the baby and you or your partner aren't ready for that reveal, SPEAK UP. You don't want to be caught off guard. Discuss this in advance so you both know where you stand on the "To know or not to know" question.

Post-visit, you're going to want to talk it all over. There's a lot to process: due dates, birthing plans, possible concerns from the doc. This isn't just her homework; it's yours too. Look stuff up, get educated, and actively participate in making decisions.

Also, don't forget the joy in this. For all the talk of tests, screenings, and other medical-sounding stuff, remember why you're doing it all. You're about to be a dad, and that's pretty incredible. Each visit is a step closer to meeting the newest member of your family.

Keep your eyes on the prize; by that, I mean your soon-to-be incredible kid. You're building something amazing here—one doctor's visit at a time.

1.6 All About Cravings: The Good, The Bad, The Pickles

So, are you enjoying this rollercoaster yet? Buckle up, buddy, because we're about to dive into the Wonderland of Pregnancy Cravings. This isn't your run-of-the-mill late-night fast-food urge; we're talking about a whole new level of food fascination. But it's not just her journey down the rabbit hole of odd cravings—oh no, you're coming along for the ride.

First, you need to understand that pregnancy cravings are not made up. They're as real as your Uncle Bob's fishing stories, maybe even more real. Your partner might suddenly have an intense desire for foods she never even liked before. It's like a tiny alien invader took over her taste buds. Should you accept it, your mission is to be the Craving Fulfiller.

What does that mean? Well, you could find yourself dispatched on an emergency mission for chocolate ice cream at midnight or driving across town because only a specific brand of pickle will do. I know it sounds nuts, but cravings are unpredictable. And don't even think about returning with a different brand or a "close-enough" substitute. If she wants Greek yogurt with honey, don't return triumphantly with regular yogurt. You'll never hear the end of it.

Now, you might wonder, are all these cravings okay? Do I need to intervene? Look, unless she's nibbling on chalk or wanting to chomp down a bar of soap (yes, some cravings can get that weird, and they're usually a sign to check in with the doc), your role is support, not food police. That said, if you notice that all the cravings lean toward items high in sugar, salt, or stuff generally found at a carnival food stand, maybe gently suggest some healthier options. Keyword here: gently.

And, hey, don't miss out on the fun. Share a sundae or dive into that bag of spicy chips. As much as she might be experiencing the brunt of this cravings game, there's no reason you can't indulge a little yourself. Just remember, when it comes to satisfying these cravings, you're the man for the job.

1.7 Mom's Mood Swings: How to Navigate the Emotional Seas

Ahoy, Captain! Set sail because we're navigating some choppy waters today—the emotional seas of pregnancy. If you haven't already noticed, pregnancy can be like a drama-filled movie with suspense, joy, and, yes, a few tears. No need to grab a life vest just yet; you can handle these waves if you know what you're doing.

First, let's clarify one thing: emotional fluctuations are just part of the pregnancy deal. Don't take it personally. Hormones are running the show right now, and they're as predictable as a coin toss. She's giggling over a cat video one moment, and the next, she's tearing up at a laundry detergent commercial. No, it doesn't make sense—but yes, it's your life now.

So, how do you deal with this emotional roller coaster? Rule number one: Listen. I can't stress this enough. Whether she's elated, sad, or irritable, the best thing you can do is be a solid sounding board. Nod, make the right noises, and, for the love of all things dad-like, do not offer solutions unless she specifically asks for them. Most of the time, she needs you to listen.

Rule number two: Be flexible. If you had plans for a dinner date and she's just not feeling it, don't push it. Be ready to adapt. If that means a night in with her favorite take-out and a rom-com, so be it. Your flexibility now earns you invaluable brownie points and a happier, less stressed partner.

What happens if I end up on the receiving end of these emotional ups and downs? Good question. Honestly, it might happen. If it does, remember it's not really about you. Keep your cool and avoid escalating the situation. This is not the time for your ego to enter the stage. Walk away if you have to, but do it respectfully and give it another go later when the waters have calmed.

Rule number three, which is a biggie: Check in on her emotional well-being. Sure, a mood swing here and there is to be expected, but if you notice persistent signs of depression or anxiety, it's essential to address them. Suggest talking to a healthcare provider; they can navigate these emotional seas much better than Dr. Google.

Alright, First Mate, you're getting a good sea leg for managing these emotional swells. Just keep your eyes on the horizon—there's land in sight, also known as the arrival of your new family member. For now, your job is to keep the ship steady and stay the course.

1.8 The Parenting Classes Debate: To Go or Not to Go

We're about to tackle a question that's probably been bugging you—or will soon enough: Should you attend parenting classes or not? You might think you've got this whole dad thing in the bag because you've successfully kept a houseplant alive or coached a Little League team, but trust me, nothing quite prepares you for the "Big League" of fatherhood.

First, let's get one thing out of the way: attending parenting classes doesn't mean you're clueless or incompetent. Think of it more like spring training for the upcoming major league event. Even pros go through training, right? The point is there's always something to learn.

The first type of class you might consider is a childbirth prep class. A good childbirth class won't just teach breathing techniques; it will also cover labor signs, when to head to the hospital, and your role in the whole shebang. You'll walk away feeling more like a co-pilot and less like excess baggage.

Then there are the baby care basics: diapering, feeding, and the dreaded midnight swaddle. If the only thing you've ever swaddled is a burrito, it might be a good idea to practice with something a little more, you know, squirmy. And as for diapers, there's a technique, my friend. It's not rocket science, but a class can give you a confidence boost. You'll feel like a pit crew member at a Formula 1 race, ready to tackle any diaper change in record time.

Don't overlook classes that cover the postpartum period, either. This phase is like the fourth quarter—crunch time. Knowing how to support your partner emotionally and physically can make a world of difference. Plus, it'll help you get the hang of this co-parenting gig right out of the gate.

Now, for those of you scoffing at the idea of sitting in a classroom setting—there are online options, too. They offer the same info, but in a format you can tackle at your own pace. Just don't use that as an excuse to slack off. Whether in-person or online, ensure you're actually absorbing the material. Trust me, there won't be time for a crash course later.

Bottom line: think of parenting classes as your pregame warm-up. You wouldn't step up to bat without a few practice swings, would you?

1.9 Prepping the Nest: The Early Essentials

Hey there, Bob the Builder, put down that hammer for a second. Before diving headfirst into transforming that old storage room into a nursery, let's have a heart-to-heart about what you need to focus on. Yeah, nesting isn't just for the birds or the moms; dads get that itch too, and it's all good. It's your inner caveman telling you to prepare for your new family member, but let's do it 21st-century style, shall we?

The most obvious first step is the nursery. Paint, furniture, decorations—oh my! Before you splurge on a designer crib or an aquarium that plays Mozart, take a step back. Think practical. The baby won't appreciate your expensive taste, but they will appreciate a safe and cozy environment. Make sure the crib meets safety standards, and for the love of God, assemble it correctly. There's nothing like putting a crib together while your partner is in labor. Talk about stress!

Next, let's talk about the other rooms in your home. Your living room is about to become Activity Central—feedings, diaper changes, and all sorts of baby-related action. Consider setting up a mini diaper-changing station with all the necessities so you're not running laps around the house at 3 a.m. looking for wipes.

Don't forget the car! A car seat is non-negotiable, and this isn't the place to cut corners. Get a new one that meets all safety guidelines and install it well before the due date. Many local fire or police stations offer free safety checks, so take advantage of that. No one wants to be that guy fumbling with a car seat while trying to bring the baby home.

Clothing is another area that new dads often overlook. I'm talking baby clothes, not a new set of jerseys for you. Have a few different sizes on hand; babies grow faster than weeds. And remember, your little one will go through outfits like a Hollywood star on the red carpet, so ensure you have enough clothes to avoid doing laundry every two hours.

Finally, let's talk about food. If your partner plans to breastfeed, that's great—but be prepared for formula as a backup. If it's formula from the get-go, stock up, but also be flexible. Babies are finicky eaters; they haven't read the menu.

So, there you have it, the nuts and bolts of getting your place ready for its newest occupant. Remember, you don't have to go overboard. The baby won't care if their room isn't Pinterest-worthy. What matters is that it's ready, functional, and safe.

Alright, that wraps up the first chapter of our guide. Feel like you've got a handle on the basics? Ready for what comes next?

CHAPTER 2:

Trimester One: The Rollercoaster Begins

2.1 Exercise for Two: Why Both of You Should Keep Moving

Hey there, Rocky Balboa, take off those boxing gloves for a second! Today, we're talking about a different kind of training: staying active during pregnancy. You might think this is just a mom thing, but don't be fooled. You've got a role to play, too. Think of this as training for the marathon of parenting; let's get both of you off the couch and moving.

First, let's talk about the expectant mom. Exercise during pregnancy has heaps of benefits: better mood, more energy, and less discomfort. Plus, staying active can even make labor and delivery smoother. So, how can you support her? For starters, be her cheerleader, but don't be pushy. Maybe offer to go on daily walks together or join a prenatal yoga class as her plus one. Make it about spending quality time together, not just checking off a workout box.

And for you, my friend, exercise isn't just about maintaining that dad-bod or preparing for the Olympic event of baby-lifting. Staying active keeps your stress levels in check, and trust me, you want to be as Zen as possible during this journey. Working out naturally elevates your spirits, and a more joyful you is a win for everyone in the mix.

Now, you don't have to go all out and join a boot camp—unless that's your jam, then by all means, go for it. Even light to moderate exercise can make a world of difference. Consider strolls, easy-paced runs, or perhaps knocking around a couple of golf balls at the driving range.

Here's another tip: make exercise a couple's activity. Whether weekend hikes or nightly stretches, doing it together creates a sense of partnership. And let's be real: your partner might be more motivated to keep moving if you're right there with her.

If you've both been pretty sedentary, consult her healthcare provider before starting any new exercise regimen. You want to make sure you're choosing safe and appropriate activities for her current pregnancy stage.

So, put on those running shoes, dust off that yoga mat, or whatever gets you going. Keep in mind that this isn't just about physical health but also bonding as you prepare for a seismic change in your lives.

2.2 Nutrition Facts: Building a Healthy Foundation

Well, well, well, if it isn't Gordon Ramsay in the making! But before you whip up your signature beef bourguignon, let's have a real talk about nutrition. It's not just about what's on your plate anymore; it's about setting the table for two—actually, make that three.

Pregnancy nutrition isn't only a mom's concern. Your partner's diet is critical because she's building a tiny human from scratch, which requires some top-quality building blocks. But don't underestimate your role in this. Eating well isn't just supportive; it's leading by example.

Firstly, let's talk about protein. No, this isn't an excuse to chow down on burgers every night. Mix it up with fish, lean meats, and plant-based options like lentils and chickpeas. Protein is essential for the development of your little one, so ensure it's on the menu regularly.

Vegetables and fruits should be your new best friends. Fruits and vegetables are brimming with crucial vitamins and minerals, not to mention they're an excellent source of fiber that can alleviate some of the, let's say, 'gastrointestinal challenges' often experienced by expectant mothers. A bonus? If you both get into the habit of eating fruits and veggies now, you'll be more likely to offer them to your kiddo down the line.

Calcium's the next VIP at your dinner party. Dairy products are a go-to, but if lactose isn't on your love list, there are plenty of other options: think leafy greens and fortified plant milks. Calcium is key for building strong bones both for mom and baby.

Now, let's talk hydration. Water is crucial during pregnancy—for amniotic fluid, increasing blood volume, and keeping everything flowing smoothly, if you catch my drift. Set a good example by ditching the sodas and making water your main squeeze.

And hey, I get that cravings can turn even the best-laid meal plans upside down. Whether it's midnight ice cream runs or pickles for breakfast, indulging occasionally is fine. Just don't make a habit of it. Remember, you're not eating for two but setting the tone for a balanced family life.

So there you go, a crash course in Nutritional Wisdom 101. And if you're the one doing the cooking, now's a perfect time to start experimenting with healthy recipes. Believe me, getting a handle on some staple healthy dishes now will be a game-changer when you're running on fumes and balancing fatherhood responsibilities down the road.

Ready to head to the grocery store and fill that cart with some good stuff? Or shall we saunter to the next part?

2.3 The Waiting Game: Why Patience is Your New Best Friend

Ah, patience. That old virtue that sounds so simple but is hard as nails to practice, especially when you're buzzing with anticipation and deadlines at work are breathing down your neck. But, my friend, if ever there was a time to develop this skill, it's now.

You might think waiting for the big day is like waiting for a pot to boil—painfully slow, with moments where you're convinced time has actually stopped. And let's not even mention those final weeks; they can feel like a lifetime! But here's the thing: patience isn't just about making it through the long days and even longer nights without losing your marbles. It's about learning to navigate this new chapter in your life without sweating the small stuff.

Firstly, medical appointments. You're going to sit in a lot of waiting rooms. I mean, a lot. Remember, time spent in a waiting room is time to relax, catch up, or even read another chapter of this fine book. It's also an opportunity to support your partner, making her feel less alone in this journey. So, smile, grab a dated magazine, and make the best of it.

Then there's the mood swings—from both her and you. Hormones are having a party, and Patience got an invite. Your partner might snap over something trivial. You might get irritated because she forgot to buy milk. Deep breaths. In the grand scheme of things, these are tiny bumps on the road to parenthood.

Patience is also your ally when it comes to planning. You'd want to buy everything for the baby, decorate the nursery, and have all the logistics sorted out yesterday. Easy there, Turbo. Some things need to unfold in their own time. That crib will get assembled, the baby shower will happen, and yes, you'll eventually decide on a name you can both live with.

And let's not forget about the labor. When the moment finally arrives, labor can be quick or take its sweet time. You'll need to be there, supportive and calm, no matter how long it takes. Remember, she's doing the heavy lifting; the least you can do is be patient and present.

So, take it from an old hand: patience isn't just a virtue; it's your new best friend. Lean into it, and you'll find that the whole experience—from pregnancy to labor to those first weeks at home—becomes a lot more manageable.

How's the patience meter holding up? Ready to dive into the next paragraph and see what else you've got to prepare for?

2.4 The Ultrasound: A Snapshot into Your Future

Well, look who's ready for his first movie premiere! But this isn't a Hollywood blockbuster; it's something far more epic—an ultrasound. You're about to get a sneak peek at your future, and trust me; it's way better than any trailer you've ever seen.

Let's get something straight: the ultrasound isn't just a photo op. It's a critical medical exam that checks how your baby is developing. It's where you'll find out things like whether your kiddo's got the right number of fingers and toes or if they're sucking their thumb. It's also where some folks find out the sex of the baby—if they choose to, of course. But above all, it's literally a chance to see your future taking shape.

Be there. That's tip number one. Unless there's an unmovable obstacle like a work emergency, ensure you're in that room. Your presence is more than symbolic; it's a source of support for your partner and a way to connect with this life-changing event.

While you're at it, bring some tissues. No, I'm not joking. The first time you see that little blip on the screen and hear the heartbeat, it can stir up some serious emotions. If you find your eyes suddenly spring a leak, don't sweat it. It happens to the best of us. It's like your heart suddenly understands the gravity of what's coming, and there's something undeniably magical about it.

Don't be surprised if the ultrasound tech starts throwing around terms like "femur length" or "amniotic fluid index." They're not trying to baffle you; it's part of their routine checks. Feel free to ask questions if you're confused about what's happening. It's your baby, after all, and you've got every right to know what's going on.

Oh, and a quick heads-up: your baby might not be camera-ready. Sometimes, the little one decides it's nap time or simply refuses to shift into a good position for a photo. Don't fret if the first images aren't crystal clear. There will be other opportunities; each ultrasound is just one piece of the puzzle.

Get a printout or digital copy if you can. This is the first tangible evidence of your child's existence, something you can show off to family and friends. Plus, it's a great addition to the baby book you might create down the line.

Well, that's a wrap on ultrasounds. But don't close the curtain just yet; there's more to come in this dad-to-be journey. Shall we proceed?

2.5 Pregnancy Fails: Common Mistakes New Dads Make

No one expects you to be a flawless dad-to-be straight out of the gate. Heck, if fatherhood came with a manual, I wouldn't be here giving you the lowdown. But there are some classic missteps that many new dads make, and I'm here to help you sidestep those pitfalls.

First up: underestimating morning sickness. Fellas, this isn't just a cutesy term for a mild tummy upset. For some women, it's a 24/7 rollercoaster of nausea. So, if your partner says she's not feeling well, take her seriously.

Next, going overboard with the dad jokes. Look, humor is a fantastic way to cope with stress, but timing is everything. Cracking a joke while she's going through a hormone surge or feeling anxious might not go down well. Read the room—or, in this case, the mom-to-be.

Here's a biggie: missing doctor's appointments. I get it. Life's busy, and sometimes it feels like you need to clone yourself to get everything done. But these prenatal checkups are non-negotiable. They're not just for her but for you and the baby, too. So clear your calendar and be there, not just physically but emotionally as well.

And finally, don't be that guy who says, "We're pregnant." While it's lovely that you want to share in the journey, let's not forget who's doing the heavy lifting—literally. Keep the focus on her. Yes, this is a partnership, but she's the one whose body is a construction zone for the next nine months.

Alright, have we dodged some bullets? Feeling a bit more prepared to tackle the landmines of pregnancy without stepping on one? Good. Let's keep those dad skills sharpening, shall we?

2.6 Understanding Hormones: A Crash Course

Buckle up, buddy, because we're diving into the mysterious world of hormones. Think of them as the invisible conductors orchestrating this whole pregnancy symphony. Don't worry; I won't turn this into a biochemistry lecture. Just some basics to help you understand what's going on behind the scenes.

First off, let's talk estrogen and progesterone. These are the big kahunas of pregnancy hormones. They're in charge of everything from helping the placenta grow to preparing your partner's breasts for breastfeeding. So, if you hear these names tossed around, know they're a pretty big deal.

Next up is a hormone known as human chorionic gonadotropin, or hCG for short. It's the one that pregnancy tests are designed to detect, and its main role is to support the embryo in the crucial early weeks. Its job is to ensure the embryo gets what it needs in those early weeks. This little hormone is a key player in the first trimester.

Oh, and let's not forget relaxin. This one's pretty chill; its primary role is to relax the uterine muscles to prevent contractions in early pregnancy. But it also works on other muscles and joints, making them more flexible, and it prepares your partner's body for childbirth. So, if she's suddenly more bendy or complains about loose-feeling joints, you can tip your hat to relaxin.

Why do you need to know all this? Because these hormones are also responsible for mood swings, food aversions, and even that notorious morning sickness. Having a rudimentary understanding can help you anticipate some of the ups and downs your partner might experience.

So, the next time your partner is sobbing over a commercial or refusing to eat her once-favorite meal, don't take it personally. It's the hormones talking. And let's be real—you're not exactly running on an even keel these days, either. Stress and anticipation also affect you, even if you don't have the hormonal whirlwind as an excuse.

One last tip: steer clear of blaming everything on hormones when talking to your partner. While it's true they're pulling a lot of strings, saying "It's just your hormones" could get you in more trouble than forgetting to take out the trash.

Okay, fellow dad-in-training, we're one step closer to understanding the mysteries of pregnancy. Ready to continue? The next chapter has some vital intel you won't want to miss.

2.7 Time Management: Balancing Work, Pregnancy, and Sleep

Alright, Einstein, let's talk about the theory of relativity—or, more precisely, how time seems to stretch and contract when you're expecting a baby. There's work to do, doctors' appointments to attend, and let's not forget you still need to catch some Zs somewhere in there. Balancing your schedule during these nine months can feel like spinning plates while walking a tightrope. But don't worry, I've got some pointers for you.

First and foremost, you need a shared calendar, my friend. Whether it's a good old-fashioned wall calendar or a digital one that sends you notifications, this thing will become your bible. Mark off key dates—doctor's appointments, baby classes, deadlines for buying baby gear—and ensure you both can access it. That way, you're on the same page, literally.

Now, about work. This is a good time to start having conversations with your employer about paternity leave. Know your rights and options. Also, be transparent about doctor's appointments and other commitments. A heads-up to your boss and teammates can go a long way in smoothing out your schedule and theirs. And let's be honest, you'll want to save those vacation days for when the baby arrives, so plan wisely.

Don't forget to carve out some time for just the two of you. Look, "date night" doesn't have to mean a candlelit dinner at a fancy restaurant. It could be as simple as watching a movie together or going for a walk. The goal is to maintain your relationship amidst the whirlwind of pregnancy. You can't effectively be there for your partner if your relationship isn't stable, much like how you need to secure your oxygen mask before helping others.

Sleep. You remember what that is, right? Here's the deal: your partner will be fatigued from growing a human being. She'll need more sleep. You, on the other hand, might find your sleep disrupted by stress or late-night Google sessions on "How to swaddle a baby." Try to establish good sleep hygiene. Go to bed at a reasonable time, keep screens out of the bedroom, and make it a sanctuary for rest.

Lastly, it's okay to say no to things. Pre-pregnancy, you might have been up for a weekend trip or a night out with the boys. But priorities shift. It's okay to decline invitations or to postpone plans. Anyone who's been through this journey will understand.

Time management is a crucial skill you'll need, not just for these nine months but for the lifetime that follows. But for now, focus on the immediate future—like the next sub-chapter in this guide.

2.8 Prepping Pets: The New Arrival

Animals, especially dogs and cats, are more perceptive than we give them credit for. They can sense change, even if they don't understand it. Start by slowly introducing new scents to be associated with the baby—like baby lotion or the specific brand of diapers you'll be using. Place these near the pet's bed or favorite hangout spot.

Here's another tip: if your dog or cat is used to being the center of attention, start varying your attention now to help them adjust. Spend time cuddling, but also practice periods where they are not the focal point. This can help reduce jealousy or anxiety when the baby becomes the unavoidable center of attention.

After the baby arrives, think about sending a piece of fabric or clothing the baby has used back to the house. Let your pet sniff it and get accustomed to it. This can help them recognize the baby as a member of the pack when you bring them home.

And once the baby's here? Always supervise any interaction with the baby and allow them to get used to their new family member gradually.

Let's be clear: there will be bumps in the road: jealousy, behavioral changes, maybe even a bit of acting out. But remember, you're building a family here, a team. Every member needs time to adjust to their new role.

2.9 Ending the Trimester: One Down, Two to Go

Well, well, well, look at you! You've made it through the first trimester. Give yourself a pat on the back, my friend. The first stretch of this pregnancy journey is often the most jarring, filled with new experiences and lessons. But don't crack open the non-alcoholic champagne just yet; you've still got two more trimesters to navigate. Here's what you need to know as you close out the first chapter of this adventure.

First off, reflect a bit. Take some time to think about what you've learned so far. How are you feeling? Is this whole "about-to-be-a-dad" thing getting more real for you? Now's the time to look back at the highs and lows and mentally prep for what's next. Trust me, being a little introspective can give you some valuable perspective.

If you haven't yet, this is an excellent time to document the journey. Some guys keep a journal; others make short video clips. Why do this? Well, in the blur of sleepless nights and diaper changes, it's easy to forget these early days. You might appreciate having something to look back on. Plus, it could be a great keepsake for your kid one day.

By now, you've likely been to a couple of doctor's appointments, and maybe you've even had the first ultrasound. Those images are your sneak peek into who's coming into your life, so hold onto them. Trust me, they're more than just fridge material—they're your first real connection to your child.

Now, a word on milestones. You might find out the gender of the baby soon if you haven't already. Whether you plan to do a gender reveal or keep it low-key is entirely up to you. Either way, finding out if you're having a boy or a girl can make this whole thing even more tangible.

Don't forget to check in with your partner. How's she doing as the first trimester winds down? Her body's going through massive changes, and the emotional rollercoaster is far from over. Keep the lines of communication open, and ensure you're both sharing how you feel. It's the two of you in this together, after all.

And lastly, brace yourself. If you thought the first trimester was a whirlwind, you ain't seen nothing yet. More changes, more preparations, and yes, more responsibilities are coming your way. But guess what? You're ready for it—or at least, as ready as any first-time dad can be.

And there we have it, the end of Chapter 2! You've navigated the minefield of the first trimester and lived to tell the tale. I hope you're pumped because the adventure's just getting started. Onward to the next chapter, shall we?

CHAPTER 3:

Trimester Two: The Eye of the Storm

3.1 The Gender Reveal: How to Handle the Big News

So, you're approaching the grand moment where you find out if you're having a little prince or princess. In a world filled with gender reveal parties that sometimes end up in tabloid headlines (don't be that guy, please), how you choose to handle this monumental news is up to you. In this sub-chapter, let's break down your options and how to navigate the emotional landscape that comes with them.

Firstly, the good old-fashioned doctor's office reveal. It's just the two of you in a dimly lit room, staring at a screen that looks like an '80s video game. The technician moves the wand, and boom, you find out if it's a boy or a girl. This moment, my friend, is intimate and personal. There's something special about finding out in real-time, with just your partner beside you—no fanfare, no fireworks, just raw emotion.

If you're the type that loves a spectacle, then the gender reveal party

25

might be your jam. Picture this: balloons, confetti, cake, the whole shebang. Everyone you love gathered in one place, the tension building, and then a grand spectacle to reveal blue or pink. Just remember, the larger the audience, the higher the emotional stakes. Are you both okay with showing raw reactions in front of friends and family? Think it through.

Some couples opt for something in between. They find out the gender and then do a private reveal for just themselves—maybe a cake you both cut into or a box you open together. It's a moment shared just between you two, but with a sprinkle of ceremony.

Now, let's talk emotional prep. Whether you've had visions of playing catch with a son or having tea parties with a daughter, finding out the gender can bring up a lot of feelings. Maybe you're ecstatic, or perhaps there's a twinge of gender disappointment. Guess what? Both are okay. What's crucial is to talk about it, process it, and then embrace the reality of who's coming into your life.

Oh, and a quick note on sharing the news: you don't have to. Seriously. If you want to keep it under wraps until the birth, that's your prerogative. People will ask, of course, because people are nosy like that. A polite "We're keeping it a surprise" usually does the trick.

Lastly, whatever the gender, remember this is your child—a unique individual who will have their own likes, dislikes, and personality traits. The gender might give you some societal framework, but the kid will be whoever they're going to be.

And that's a wrap on handling the big gender reveal. Remember, there's no right or wrong way to go about it; it's all about what feels authentic to you and your partner. So, what's next on our journey? Stick around to find out.

3.2 The Babymoon: A Last Hurrah or a Hassle?

Ah, the babymoon. A term that didn't exist a generation ago but is now as common as morning sickness and weird cravings. For the uninitiated, a babymoon is like a honeymoon, but instead of celebrating being newlyweds, you're celebrating the upcoming birth of your child. Sounds dreamy, right? But let's be real—is it a heavenly last hurrah or more of a logistical hassle? Let's dive in.

First off, let's talk timing. The second trimester is generally the Goldilocks zone for a babymoon. Why? Your partner's likely past the queasy stage but not yet at the point where travel is a challenge—or downright uncomfortable. Plus, most airlines have restrictions on flying during the later stages of pregnancy, so you're in a sweet spot.

Now, on to the destination. We've all seen the Instagram posts—exotic locales, serene beaches, couples beaming under the tropical sun. It's lovely, but maybe not practical for everyone, especially if finances are a consideration. The good news? A babymoon doesn't have to be extravagant. Even a staycation can achieve the same goal: quality time together before your duo becomes a trio.

If you opt for travel, there are a few things to keep in mind. First, consult your healthcare provider. Make sure travel is safe for both mom and baby. Then, consider the facilities and healthcare available at your chosen destination. It's a good idea to know where the nearest hospital is, just in case. Also, pack wisely. Bring any meds and prenatal vitamins you'll need. Maybe even pack a pillow from home to make sleeping more comfortable for your partner.

Alright, let's address the elephant in the room—the hassle factor. Traveling while pregnant can have its share of inconveniences, from frequent bathroom breaks to limited food options. Not to mention, some pregnant women experience heightened senses, so the smell of airport food or car exhaust could be nauseating. Is it worth it? Only you two can decide.

The biggest takeaway from a babymoon should be relaxation and connection. This is one of the last times you'll have each other's undivided attention for a while. So, whether it's in Bali or your backyard, make it about you two.

And hey, even if you skip the babymoon entirely, find other ways to connect. Date nights, long walks, or simply binge-watching your favorite series together can offer the same emotional benefits without the need for sunscreen or passports.

3.3 The Belly Touchers: Managing Unwanted Attention

We're entering strange territory now. Imagine you're strolling through the grocery store, minding your own business, when out of nowhere, someone—maybe even a complete stranger—reaches out and rubs your partner's belly like she's a magical Buddha granting wishes. Sounds awkward, right? Welcome to the world of belly touchers. Let's talk strategy for managing these well-meaning but often intrusive folks.

First, let's understand the psychology—without diving into deep psychology, of course. Pregnancy is fascinating. A new life is growing, and people are naturally drawn to it. It's like the world's most amazing science project everyone wants to participate in. But here's the catch: while the belly is out there for the world to see, it's still a part of your partner's body, and boundaries should be respected.

Now, on to you, the dad-to-be. You've got a role in this, believe it or not. Your job is to be the buffer, the guardian of the belly, if you will. When you see that hand reaching out for a pat, a well-timed "Hey, how's it going?" can divert the trajectory. Just your presence alone can serve as a deterrent.

For those closer to you—family and friends who should know better but sometimes don't—it might take a direct conversation. A simple "We're trying to be cautious about germs" or "She's not feeling great, maybe skip the belly rub today" can work wonders. It sets boundaries without making things overly awkward.

If your partner is the outspoken type, she might prefer to handle these situations herself. Every woman is different. Some don't mind the belly attention, while for others, it's a significant invasion of personal space. Ensure you and your partner are on the same page about handling these interactions. Communication is key.

But what if the belly toucher is someone you can't easily fend off, like your boss or an elderly relative? In cases like these, sometimes a little humor can diffuse the situation. A jovial "Careful, the baby kicks back!" can send the message without creating tension.

Remember, most people mean well; they're just caught up in the excitement of it all. It's up to you and your partner to set the boundaries that make you comfortable.

3.4 Baby Shopping: What You Really Need vs. What's Nice to Have

So, you've seen the baby aisle at the store, right? Adorable clothes and rows and rows of tiny little gadgets to make you wonder, "Did babies suddenly become NASA engineers?" It's a wild jungle out there, and if you're not careful, you'll walk away with an armful of stuff you didn't know existed and probably don't actually need. In this sub-chapter, we'll break down the baby essentials and the baby... well, not-so-essentials.

First up, the absolutes—the things you really can't go without. Diapers are a given; whether you go cloth or disposable, you'll need a lot. Trust me on this one. Then there's formula or breast pumps and bottles if you're going that route. And don't forget a car seat; hospitals won't let you leave without one properly installed. These are your need-to-haves; no question about them.

Now, let's get to the more nuanced stuff. Take baby clothes, for example. Sure, those tiny shoes are so cute they should be illegal, but does a newborn really need sneakers? Spoiler alert: they don't. Onesies, sleepers, and maybe a couple of cute outfits for photos or outings should suffice in the beginning. Babies grow so fast that half the stuff will still have tags on when they've outgrown them.

Swings, white noise machines, electronic diaper trash cans—these are what I'd call "luxury items." They're nice to have and can make life easier, but you'll survive without them. If you're working on a budget, these are the things you can likely do without or pick up later once you've got the hang of this parenting gig.

Now, for the love of your wallet, don't underestimate the power of hand-me-downs and second-hand shops. Babies don't know that their stroller isn't the latest model or that their crib has seen two cousins before them. Used items can be a real budget-saver if they're safe and meet current safety standards.

So, how do you figure out what you actually need? Talk to friends or family who've recently had kids. Folks often enjoy sharing their wisdom on these matters, and you can gain valuable insights from another person's successes and failures. Also, there are tons of checklists available online. Just remember, every family is different. What's essential for one might be completely unnecessary for another.

And there it is, the baby shopping decoder ring you didn't know you needed. With this guide, you can navigate those baby aisles like a pro and come home with just what you need, avoiding the wallet-draining pitfalls that scare so many new parents. What's next on the docket? You'll have to stick around to find out.

3.5 Prepping for Parental Leave: A Guide for Dads

Ah, parental leave, that magical time when you get to step away from work for a bit to focus on your new, tiny, sleep-depriving bundle of joy. But before you start dreaming about all those cozy hours you'll spend rocking your newborn to sleep, let's get real: parental leave needs some planning, especially for dads.

First off, check your work's policy on parental leave. I know, I know, diving into HR paperwork is about as fun as assembling a crib with a missing instruction manual, but it's crucial. You need to know how much time you're allowed, whether it's paid or not, and the process for requesting the leave. Get this sorted early to avoid any last-minute surprises.

Next, have a chat with your manager. You don't want to just drop a bomb saying, "Hey boss, I'm outta here for a month, peace!" Give them ample heads-up, and offer a plan for how your responsibilities will be covered during your absence. The more prepared you appear, the smoother this will go, I promise.

Now let's talk budget. If your parental leave isn't paid, or if it's only partially paid, you'll need to crunch some numbers. Look at your savings, consider your expenses (they're about to go up, trust me), and figure out how long you can comfortably take off. It's better to sort this out now rather than when you're knee-deep in diapers and baby wipes.

Okay, on to the home front. Cook some meals to freeze, stock up on essentials, and try to tick off any lingering to-dos. Trust me, the last thing you'll want to do on your parental leave is run errands.

Last but definitely not least, set some goals for your time off. It's easy for days to blur together when you're sleep-deprived and handling a newborn. Maybe your aim is as simple as bonding with your baby, or perhaps you want to use the time to help establish a feeding and sleeping routine. Whatever it is, having a goal will give your days some structure, which can be a godsend in those chaotic first weeks.

And that's the playbook for prepping your parental leave, gents. Trust me, a little planning goes a long way. The more you sort out now, the more you'll be able to focus on what really matters when the time comes: your new family.

3.6 Feeling the Baby Kick: It's Not Sci-Fi, It's Real

We're approaching one of the most mind-blowing, awe-inspiring milestones in the pregnancy journey: the first baby kicks. No, this isn't some sci-fi movie where an alien lifeform communicates via stomach Morse code. It's your actual baby, sending you a tap-tap-tap from inside the womb. How do you prepare for this unreal experience? Let's dive in.

First of all, let's debunk a myth: not every mom-to-be feels those kicks around the same time. We're talking anywhere from 16 to 25 weeks, generally speaking. And if it's her first pregnancy, it might be later. So, don't worry if you're past some arbitrary deadline you read on an internet forum; it'll happen when it happens.

Now, when your partner does start feeling those kicks, she might not even be sure that's what she's experiencing. Early kicks often feel like gas or butterflies flitting around. Encourage her to tune into her body. Once she's sure she's feeling kicks, the next milestone is having you feel them, too.

Here's a pro tip: be patient. Early kicks are generally too soft for anyone other than the mom to feel. But as the weeks roll by, they'll get stronger. You might find yourself resting your hand on her belly for what feels like an eternity, but when you finally feel that little nudge, it's a game-changer. It makes everything more real, more immediate.

So, what do you do when you finally feel that kick? Celebrate it, obviously! This is one of the first interactions you'll have with your child. Whether you talk back, play some music, or just sit in awe is up to you. But take the moment to connect. Your baby is getting to know you, too, in their own special way.

There's also a practical side to all this. Paying attention to the baby's movements can be important for monitoring their health. Your partner might be advised to do "kick counts" later in the pregnancy to ensure everything goes well. Be involved in that. It's not just reassuring; it's responsible.

3.7 Maintaining Intimacy: Navigating the Romantic Seas

Alright, gentlemen, let's chat about something likely on your mind but maybe hasn't made it to the conversation table yet: intimacy during pregnancy. I'm not solely focusing on the physical aspects, which are certainly vital, but also on the emotional bond that sustains the romantic spark. Let's break down how to navigate these occasionally choppy waters.

First up, let's talk communication. With all the baby prep, doctor's appointments, and late-night ice cream runs, it's easy for the 'How was your day, dear?' conversations to get lost. Take time to check in with each other. It sounds simple, but a few minutes of genuine conversation can go a long way in keeping you both connected.

Now, on to the physical side of things. Pregnancy impacts everyone differently, and this includes your partner's libido. Hormones are running wild, and fatigue is a constant companion. Also, let's not forget that growing belly. It's not uncommon for one or both of you to experience a shift in your sex drive. The key is to be adaptable and understanding. Think beyond just intercourse; massages, cuddling, or even a romantic dinner can fill the gap when traditional intimacy isn't an option.

Alright, you might also be wondering about the safety of, you know, 'getting busy' during pregnancy. Here's the good news: for most pregnancies, it's absolutely safe right up until the end. Of course, consult your healthcare provider for personalized advice, especially if your partner has any complications. But generally speaking, you're in the clear.

Don't neglect the emotional aspect, either. Pregnancy is a rollercoaster, and it's not just your partner strapped in; you're riding right beside her. Take time to be affectionate. Leave a sweet note, give a random hug, or initiate an impromptu slow dance in the kitchen. These small gestures can make a world of difference.

Finally, let's talk about vulnerability. Your partner is going through a significant life change, and you are, too. It's okay to be scared, uncertain, or overwhelmed. Share those feelings with each other. Your relationship will be stronger for it, and you'll both feel less alone on this journey.

So there you have it, the lowdown on maintaining intimacy during the pregnancy adventure. It might require some adjustments, but keep your eyes on the prize. After all, your partnership is the foundation on which your new family will be built. Keep it strong.

3.8 Avoiding Toxic Conversations: What Not to Say to a Pregnant Woman

Listen up, gents. We've navigated the seas of morning sickness, sailed through the ultrasound waves, and even survived the baby-kick storms. It's time to tackle another treacherous subject: what NOT to say to a pregnant woman. Trust me, the wrong word can turn your tranquil home into the Bermuda Triangle, and no one wants to be lost at sea. Let's chart a safe course.

First on the list: commenting on her size. You might think you're being endearing with remarks like "Wow, you're getting big!" or "Are you sure it's not twins?" Trust me, you're not. Even if you find the transformations in her body during pregnancy remarkable, remember it's probably a delicate subject for her. Stick to safer waters; tell her she looks beautiful, glowing, or radiant.

Next, avoid acting like the food police. She already knows what she should and shouldn't eat during pregnancy. Unless you've suddenly gained a degree in obstetrics, steer clear of making comments about her food choices. I guarantee you, she's more in tune with her body's needs and restrictions than ever before.

Third, let's talk about labor stories. Yes, you've read about all sorts of complications online. No, you don't need to share these tales with your partner. Pregnancy already comes with its own set of worries, so adding more anxiety to the mix helps no one.

Don't offer unsolicited advice about how she should handle her pregnancy or the impending labor. There's a good chance she's already been bombarded with tips, suggestions, and recommendations from everyone. Instead, ask how you can support her. It's not about what you think she should do but what she needs from you.

Lastly, the sleep issue. If you dare to utter the words, "You should sleep now because you won't be able to later," prepare to walk the plank. She's probably not sleeping well as it is, thanks to the changing body, heartburn, or frequent trips to the bathroom. Don't rub it in. Offer to help make her comfortable instead.

There you have it, mates, the guide to avoiding toxic conversations and keeping your relationship in shipshape during pregnancy. Remember, it's a team effort. Communication is key, and a little tact can go a long way.

3.9 Your Partner's Body: Supporting Her Through

Changes

Alright, fellas, it's time for a heart-to-heart. Pregnancy isn't just about a growing belly; it's a full-body experience that will change your partner in expected and surprising ways. The transformation is real, from stretch marks to swollen ankles, and how you support her through it matters. Let's dive in, shall we?

Firstly, let's talk stretch marks. These little "tiger stripes" can appear on the belly, thighs, or even the breasts. Some women wear them as a badge of honor, while others are self-conscious about them. Your job? Be supportive and reassuring. Consider them battle scars in the noblest of all causes: bringing new life into the world. A little cocoa butter massage wouldn't hurt, either.

Next up, we have the infamous pregnancy waddle. As her belly grows, her center of gravity shifts. She might start walking differently, and hey, it's not because she's mimicking a penguin for kicks. A simple arm to hold onto while walking can make all the difference in the world. Be that arm.

Then there's the matter of swollen feet and ankles. Ah, yes, the days of sexy heels might be on hold for a while. What can you do? Get a basin of warm water, add a little Epsom salt, and offer a soothing foot soak. It's like a spa day but in the comfort of your own home. Top it off with a gentle foot massage, and you've just earned major brownie points.

Ah, the ever-changing breasts. Yes, they'll get bigger, but that's not an open invitation for inappropriate comments or unsolicited touches. They're also more sensitive and could be sore. Be aware and respectful of these changes, especially when it comes to intimacy.

And there you go, a quick but comprehensive guide on supporting your partner through the bodily changes of pregnancy. Remember, she's not just carrying your child but also the weight of all these physical adjustments. A little empathy, sensitivity, and proactive caring go a long way.

3.10 Your Mental Check-in: Keeping Stress at Bay

Gentlemen, we've spent a lot of time discussing how to be there for your partner, but let's not forget about you. While you're not carrying the baby, you're carrying your share of responsibilities, anticipations, and, yes, stresses. Your mental well-being is equally important in this nine-month journey. So, let's focus on you for a minute.

First off, it's okay to feel overwhelmed. Whether it's the baby's impending arrival, financial worries, or just the weight of becoming a dad, you're allowed to feel the pressure. The trick is not to let it consume you. Find healthy ways to blow off steam, be it a game of basketball, a solo drive, or even strumming the guitar for a few minutes.

Next, let's talk about the "Dad Bod" phenomenon. As your partner's body changes, yours might too. It's not uncommon for soon-to-be dads to gain a little sympathy weight. If this bothers you, tackle it head-on. Go for walks, hit the gym, or involve your partner in prenatal yoga. Physical activity is not just good for your body; it does wonders for your mental health too.

Now, about those sleepless nights. You might not be the one with a baby bump causing discomfort, but the weight of impending fatherhood can cause its own brand of insomnia. Insufficient sleep can trigger stress, which in turn fuels more nights of poor sleep—creating a harmful loop. Consider natural sleep aids like warm milk or herbal teas (obviously not for your partner if she's avoiding certain herbs during pregnancy) and maybe a calming nighttime routine.

Then, there's the mental load. The never-ending list of things to do before the baby arrives can be daunting. Turn this into an opportunity for bonding with your partner. Sit together and plan the chores, doctor visits, and other prep work. Divvy up the tasks. You'll feel less overwhelmed and more in control.

Lastly, let's tackle that nagging feeling of inadequacy many men feel but seldom talk about. Look, nobody expects you to be the perfect dad straight out of the gate. You'll make mistakes, and that's okay. The willingness to learn and adapt is what truly counts.

So, there you have it, your roadmap for keeping stress at bay while navigating the maze of first-time fatherhood. We've got plenty more ground to cover, but take a moment to breathe for now. Your well-being is essential to this journey, so don't neglect it. In the next chapter, we're delving into some more exciting milestones. Stay with me; we're just getting started.

CHAPTER 4:

Baby-Ready or Not: Last Month Preparations

4.1 Hospital Bag: Packing Like a Pro

Alright, lads, we've crossed the halfway point in our journey, and it's time to think logistics. The D-day—or should I say B-day—is approaching fast, and you'll need to be as prepared as a Boy Scout going on an epic adventure. The first item on the checklist is the hospital bag. We're not just throwing in a toothbrush and calling it a day; we're packing like pros. So, roll up your sleeves, and let's get to it.

First and foremost, don't underestimate the importance of snacks. You may be in that hospital room for a while, and vending machine fare won't sustain you (or your partner) through labor. Opt for high-energy, low-mess snacks like granola bars, dried fruit, and nuts. You'll thank me later.

Next up: entertainment. I'm not talking about a full-on gaming console, but labor can be a long process. Bring a book, download some movies or series episodes on your tablet, or even prep a playlist that you both love. Trust me, it'll help pass the time and can even make the experience more memorable. Just remember to bring headphones to avoid disturbing your laboring partner or the medical staff.

Ah, clothing. Bring some comfy clothes for yourself and your partner. A fresh set for her post-delivery will make her feel human again, and a clean T-shirt and shorts for you will be a welcome change. Also, bring a swimsuit; you never know if you'll end up helping your partner in a birthing pool or shower.

Documentation—yes, you'll need it. IDs, insurance info, birth plan if you have one, and emergency contact numbers should all be in an easily accessible pocket. You don't want to be scrambling to find these in the heat of the moment.

Toiletries are non-negotiable—toothbrush, toothpaste, soap, a razor, and maybe even some facial cleanser for both of you. Hospitals provide the basics, but having your own can make the experience a bit more comfortable.

Don't forget a few essential items for the newborn: a couple of onesies, some diapers, and maybe even a cute hat for those first few pictures. Hospitals usually provide these, but it's nice to have some of your own to make it personal.

Lastly, the all-important phone charger. Your phone will be your lifeline to the outside world, your camera, your clock, and your notepad. Make sure you've got the juice to keep it going.

Pack it all in a sturdy bag that's easy to carry, and voila! You're ready to head to the hospital like a seasoned pro. It might seem like a lot, but you'll be glad you're well-prepared when you're in the thick of it. On to the next topic, as the saying goes, "Proper preparation prevents poor performance."

4.2 Labor Signs: False Alarms and Real Deals

So, your bag's packed, the car tank's full, and you're pacing around like an expectant... well, father. You're all set, but how do you know when it's showtime? I've seen guys dash to the hospital for what turned out to be a case of indigestion. To save you from needless adrenaline spikes and wasted gas, let's break down the signs of labor and differentiate between the false alarms and the real deals.

Firstly, we've got the "Braxton Hicks" contractions, also known as the "practice contractions." Man, these are the ultimate trolls of pregnancy. They're the body's way of warming up for the main event. How do you differentiate them from real contractions? They're usually irregular, not very painful, and they'll go away with some change in activity or position. If your partner experiences these, don't jump the gun; it's likely a false alarm.

Now, onto the real deals. Contractions that are regular, increasing in intensity, and coming closer together are the ones to watch for. They won't go away with a change in activity and could start to radiate from the back to the front.

Contractions come in waves, peaking in intensity before fading away, and they generally get stronger, more frequent, and more regular as labor progresses.

Now, how to time them? There's an app for that, of course, but sometimes, going old-school with a stopwatch and notepad is more reliable. Note the time a contraction starts and when it stops. The time between the start of one contraction and the start of the next will give you the frequency. Also, note the duration—how long each contraction lasts. Early on, they might be erratic, lasting anywhere from 20 to 45 seconds and 15 to 30 minutes apart. But it's go-time when they're around 4 to 5 minutes apart, lasting about 40 to 60 seconds for at least an hour.

Don't panic. Seriously. I've seen dads pace around the room like caged animals, making everyone more anxious. Remember, this is a marathon, not a sprint. Your role here is to be the steadfast rock, the navigator who's done his homework, and the co-pilot who knows when it's time to head to the landing strip.

Here's a pro tip: don't rush to the hospital at the first sign of contractions unless advised by the healthcare provider. Early labor can take hours, and you might just be sent back home. Imagine the fun of doing that trip twice—or more. But if you're in doubt, or if there are other complications like bleeding or severe pain, don't hesitate. Get on that phone, talk to the healthcare provider, and make your way to the hospital if they give the green light.

Water breaking is another unmistakable sign; well, usually. Sometimes, it's a dramatic gush, like in the movies, but other times, it's just a trickle. Either way, once the water breaks, there's no turning back; your baby is getting ready for their debut.

Last but not least, there's the nesting instinct, which isn't necessarily a definitive sign of labor but an interesting phenomenon. Your partner may suddenly get the urge to clean, organize, or prepare in some way. It's like the body's way of saying, "I need to get things in order before the chaos begins." It's worth noting but not a reason to speed to the hospital.

So there you have it, fellas—the lowdown on labor signs. Knowing how to separate the false alarms from the real deals will help you remain calm and make smarter decisions when the time comes.

4.3 Nesting Overdrive: What's Normal, What's Not

Alright, we've touched upon nesting, that primal urge that hits expecting moms like a sudden revelation that the house needs to be 100% baby-ready. It's a fascinating little phenomenon, but how much nesting is too much, and when should you, as the dad-to-be, start worrying—or stop rolling your eyes? Let's dive in.

First off, some level of nesting is absolutely normal. It's nature's way of preparing both of you for the monumental change ahead. But we're generally talking about reasonable activities here: washing baby clothes, setting up the nursery, or properly installing the car seat. A bit of cleaning and organizing? All good signs. They're productive, reasonable, and hey, you might even find it a little endearing.

Then there are those moments when nesting goes into overdrive. We're talking about painting the entire house at 2 a.m. or suddenly deciding that absolutely everything needs to be re-arranged. If you find your partner scrubbing the grout with a toothbrush or vacuuming the ceiling, you might be entering the "What's Not Normal" zone.

So, what should you do if nesting shifts into the gear of irrationality? First, keep in mind that hormones are running the show. Don't react too strongly; a laid-back approach usually works best. Suggest alternatives that are safer or more reasonable. If she wants to clean, maybe steer her toward organizing baby clothes rather than climbing a ladder to dust the fan blades.

It's also essential to make sure she's not overexerting herself. Late pregnancy is not the time for heavy lifting or tackling complex home improvement projects. If she's going overboard, it might be time to call in reinforcements—like family members or friends—to get some of the tasks done more safely.

A word of caution here: if nesting behavior seems frenetic or anxiety-driven rather than purposeful and calming, it might be a sign of heightened stress or anxiety. In this case, it's advisable to consult healthcare professionals for a proper course of action.

So, gents, there's the rundown on nesting. A bit is good, a lot should raise a few eyebrows, and too much might require a gentle intervention or professional advice. As we continue this journey toward fatherhood, your role as a supportive partner becomes ever more crucial.

4.4 The 3 AM Runs: Late-night Pharmacy Visits

Ah, the 3 AM pharmacy runs. You're lounging in bed, lost in a dream where everything is serene when suddenly you're jerked awake by your partner saying she needs a very specific thing. It could be anything from an over-the-counter medication her doctor recommended to a particular brand of ginger tea that "only" the pharmacy three miles away sells. Whatever the case, welcome to the world of late-night pharmacy runs, my friend.

First off, let's keep things in perspective. It's easy to be irked by the abrupt end to your beauty sleep, but these runs are often non-negotiable. Whether it's a legitimate craving or a sudden need for a pregnancy-safe pain reliever, these late-night excursions are another test of your fatherhood preparedness.

Before you dash out, though, ensure it's something you actually need to go out for. Sometimes, a more straightforward solution might be lying around your home. If it's antacids she's after, maybe there's some baking soda in the kitchen that could serve as a temporary fix until morning. No? Alright, put on those pants; we're going for a ride.

Dress comfortably but appropriately. I know it's the middle of the night and you just want to get this over with, but you never know who you might run into or what situation may arise. Plus, many pharmacies have security cameras, and you don't want to be that guy who becomes a viral meme because he wore his boxers inside-out to the store.

Also, make a list before heading out. It's not just about what she asked you for; think about other things that might be needed soon. Grab some extra diapers, wipes, or whatever else is on the near-future shopping list. This is about being efficient with your late-night adventures.

Drive carefully. I know we covered safe driving when heading to the hospital, but it bears repeating. Your mental faculties aren't at 100% when you've been woken up at an ungodly hour. Be extra cautious, especially if the roads are empty; other late-night drivers might not be as responsible as you are.

Lastly, keep a sense of humor about the whole thing. These late-night outings might seem inconvenient now, but they'll make for fantastic stories later. Plus, your willingness to make these runs is a solid display of your commitment. Brownie points, buddy, brownie points.

The 3 AM pharmacy runs are an unexpected rite of passage on your road to fatherhood. It's practice for all those times your future child will have you up at odd hours.

4.5 Transportation: Getting to the Hospital Safely

So, you've got the signs of labor down, packed bags, and somewhat survived the nesting phase. Now, let's talk about the journey to the hospital. I've heard stories, man, of couples arriving at the hospital in anything from a limo to a bicycle—don't be those guys. Let's get into how to make this ride safe, timely, and free of unnecessary drama.

First things first: know your route. Yeah, I know, we've got GPS and all that fancy tech, but let's not underestimate the power of knowing where you're going beforehand. Do a few dry runs if you must, and take into account the time of day when traffic could be a nightmare. Knowing alternate routes is also a game-changer. You don't want to be stuck in traffic while your partner's contractions are coming faster than ads on a free streaming service.

Next, have the car ready. Keep that gas tank full as you approach the due date, and maybe even throw a couple of towels and a waterproof sheet in the backseat, just in case. The movies make it look funny, but giving birth in a car isn't the ideal scenario for anyone involved. Make sure your vehicle is reliable—if your car has been acting up, now's the time to fix it or arrange for a backup plan.

Let's talk about the speed. This is where a lot of new dads mess up. They hit the gas pedal like they're auditioning for a Fast & Furious sequel. Relax, speedster. Driving recklessly endangers everyone involved and can escalate an already tense situation. The goal is to get to the hospital safely, not win an imaginary race.

While driving, keep the atmosphere as calm as possible. Put on some soothing music if it helps, or engage in light conversation to distract your partner from her discomfort. Avoid honking and aggressive driving; it won't make things go any faster and will only increase stress levels.

And for those who don't own a car—no worries. Secure a list of trustworthy cab companies or pre-schedule transportation with a loved one or acquaintance. Public transport is usually not recommended, but hey, if you're in a city where it's super-efficient, then who am I to stop you? Just ensure it's a practical option to get there quickly and safely. A bit of planning can remove a huge chunk of stress from this monumental day.

4.6 The Birth Plan: Flexible but Prepared

Ah, the birth plan. This is your game plan, your blueprint, your script for how you'd "like" the big day to unfold. Notice how I emphasize "like." If pregnancy and parenthood teach you anything, it's the art of flexibility. But hey, that doesn't mean you shouldn't have a plan in place; you just need to be prepared for some on-the-fly adjustments.

Firstly, involve your partner in crafting this plan. I mean, she's the star of the show, after all. You're more like the director who ensures everything is in place for her to shine. Discuss everything from what kind of atmosphere you both want in the delivery room—music or no music, lights dimmed or full blaze—to who should be there. Grandma might be over the moon about witnessing the birth, but if the mom-to-be isn't comfortable with an audience, then it's a no-go. Sorry, Grandma.

Now, medical choices. Epidural, natural birth, C-section—these are things you should research together. Both of you should be comfortable with these decisions but also be prepared for surprises. Childbirth has a way of laughing in the face of your carefully laid plans.

Keep a copy of your birth plan handy. Make it easily accessible, maybe even stick it on the fridge. Also, ensure the closest people involved—like your parents or your best mate—know where to find it. This way, if you're too caught up in the whirlwind of labor to remember details, they can step in and advocate for you and your partner. The birth plan is your compass, but you're the one steering the ship, and sometimes, you'll have to sail against the wind.

4.7 Backup Team: Enlisting Family and Friends for Support

Okay, lads, it's time to talk about your bench players. You might think you've got this whole birthing thing under control. You're the main man, the number one supporter, the go-to guy, right? Well, here's the truth—sometimes, even the star player needs a break or, God forbid, gets sidelined due to unexpected circumstances. That's when your backup team comes into play.

Think about it. You're running on fumes, haven't slept properly, and the vending machine coffee is no longer cutting it. Or maybe your partner's labor is stretching over hours and even days. You could be a superhero, but even superheroes have sidekicks. So, who are you going to call? No, not Ghostbusters. It's your backup team of family and friends.

First off, decide who makes the cut. Who do you and your partner feel comfortable having in this intimate setting? Trust me, the delivery room is no place for casual acquaintances or that chatty neighbor who can't keep a secret. You need people who can offer emotional and, sometimes, physical support. Maybe it's your sister who's had three kids and can offer some practical advice, or your best mate who can make a quick run to grab fresh clothes or food.

Now, assign roles. I'm not saying you have to go all military drill sergeant on them, but a bit of organization can go a long way. Maybe your mom is great at meal prep; she could be in charge of making sure you guys are eating right during those hectic days. Perhaps your buddy is a logistics wizard; he could handle driving duties.

Don't forget to prepare these MVPs for their roles. Share the birth plan, fill them in on your partner's wishes and needs, and make sure they understand any medical jargon or procedures that might come up. Knowledge is power, and the more your backup team knows, the better they can support you.

Also, brief them on the do's and don'ts. Tell them it's not helpful to bombard you with questions or messages asking for updates every five minutes. Their job is to ease the pressure, not add to it.

Now, what if you're a private person and the idea of a backup team isn't appealing? That's cool. Just ensure you've got other support systems in place, whether it's an online community or reliable literature to guide you through the process. But, honestly, having at least one or two folks you can count on can be a game-changer.

4.8 The Waiting Room: How to Kill Time Without Losing Your Mind

Ah, the waiting room—the purgatory of hospitals. It's where time seems to stand still, and your mind races faster than a Formula 1 car on the final lap. You've done your bit in the delivery room, and now you're here, waiting for news, any news. Maybe they've kicked you out during a medical procedure, or you're letting your partner rest. Either way, you'll have to learn the art of waiting without losing your marbles.

First things first, let's tackle the beast of boredom. Look, I know we live in an age where our phones serve as gateways to unlimited entertainment. But have you ever noticed that despite this, waiting rooms still somehow turn us into fidgety, impatient messes? What you need is a strategy, mate.

Start with something simple, like a good book. It's an escape hatch from reality. If reading's not your jam, how about podcasts? There's a podcast out there for everyone, from sports enthusiasts to history buffs. Headphones in, world out. Just ensure to keep an ear open for any updates from the medical staff.

Another way to kill time is to write. Take a small notebook with you and jot down your thoughts and fears, or even start penning a letter to your unborn child. Trust me, it can be therapeutic and may offer you a chance to organize those swirling thoughts.

Stay connected but not glued to your phone. A quick text or call to your backup team to keep them in the loop is great, but avoid the black hole of social media. Your nerves are already on edge; you don't need to add the anxiety that can come from scrolling through other people's highlight reels.

Get up, stretch, walk around. Your body will thank you for a little bit of movement, and so will your mind.

Lastly, consider striking up a conversation with other folks in the waiting room. Chances are they're going through a similar emotional rollercoaster, and sometimes, a little small talk can be a welcome distraction for both parties.

The waiting room doesn't have to be this dreaded vortex where time and sanity disappear. With some prep and the right mindset, you'll come out the other side ready for action.

CHAPTER 5:

D-Day: The Birth Experience

5.1 The Hospital Tour: Knowing the Battlefield

Now, don't go into this battle unprepared; you wouldn't walk into a football game without knowing the field, would you? That's why a hospital tour is a must-do pitstop before the main event. Trust me, navigating a hospital when you're cool as a cucumber is much easier than figuring it out when you're in go-time mode.

Alright, pencil it in. Most hospitals offer tours for expecting parents. You'll usually wander through maternity, see where the magic happens in the delivery rooms, and get a sneak peek at the nursery where your mini-me will make their first public appearance. Hospitals love this stuff; it's like their version of an open house, but with more latex gloves and less awkward small talk.

Why is this important, you ask? Well, first off, it's about logistics. Knowing where to park, which elevator to take, and where the cafeteria is (trust me, you'll need to refuel) can cut out a lot of unnecessary stress. Imagine being the guy who gets lost and ends up in the orthopedic wing while his partner is about to give birth. Don't be that guy.

Also, seeing the place in advance gives you a tactical advantage. Knowing the terrain lets you be more focused and present when the action kicks off. You'll know where the bathrooms are, where to find the ice chips, and, heck, even where they stash the extra pillows.

Now, while on this tour, pay attention to the vibe. Hospitals can have a different feel. Some are like luxury hotels with birthing pools and mood lighting. Others are no-nonsense medical fortresses. Get a sense of what your partner might like or dislike. Is it too clinical? Too woo-woo? This is good recon for any last-minute game-time decisions.

Questions! Don't forget to ask questions. Ask about visitor policies, Wi-Fi (for those all-important birth announcements), and what you can bring with you. Oh, and ask where dads like you can catch a bit of shut-eye during the labor marathon. You want to be rested and ready for the fourth quarter, my man.

All in all, this is your scouting mission, so make it count. Trust me, when the big day comes, and you're navigating those hallways like an old pro, you'll thank me. You might not get a medal for bravery, but hey, being the reliable guy who knows his way around? That's its own kind of heroism, buddy. So lace up those boots, soldier, and let's recon this place. On to the next part!

5.2 Roles and Responsibilities: Your Job During Labor

Hey, hey! Still with me? Great! You've got the lay of the land. Now, let's talk about what you're actually supposed to be doing on D-day. Yeah, I get it; it's easy to feel a bit sidelined during labor. After all, you're not the one pushing out a tiny human. But make no mistake, you've got a role to play, and it's more important than you think.

Think of yourself as the co-pilot. You're not flying the plane, but you're handling communications, managing instruments, and, for the love of all things holy, making sure the pilot doesn't have to ask for a glass of water. Your job description? Simple. Be helpful, be supportive, and stay the heck out of the way when you need to.

Let's break it down, shall we?

First off, you're a timekeeper. Contractions? Yeah, there's an app for that. Download one ahead of time and know how to use it. Timing contractions helps you and the medical staff understand how far along things are. Plus, it gives you something to focus on, so you're not just standing there like a bump on a log.

Second, you're a DJ. No, seriously. Your partner might want some soothing tunes, or maybe she's the "give me death metal or give me death" type. You won't know unless you've talked about it beforehand, so make sure you've got a playlist ready to roll.

Third, you're the Advocate-in-Chief. If your partner is too busy focusing on, you know, the minor task of birthing a child, she might need you to speak up for her. Know her birth plan, know what she's comfortable with, and don't be afraid to be her voice if things get hectic.

Lastly, you're the Emotional Support Human. Sounds cheesy, but don't underestimate the power of a well-timed joke, a hand to squeeze, or even just being a familiar face in a room full of strangers wearing scrubs. Your presence alone is reassuring.

Remember, pal, you're not just a spectator. You're part of the team, and every team needs a utility player who can do a little bit of everything. So get in there, be useful, and most importantly, be there. Your partner will appreciate it, and hey, you might even earn yourself some bragging rights.

Alright, feeling more equipped for the task? Good!

5.3 Epidurals, Natural Birth, and C-Sections: The Different Paths

Now that you know you're not just an extra on the set but a bona fide supporting actor, let's dig into the various scenarios you might face in the delivery room. Think of this as choosing your game plan. Whether it's running the ball, passing, or a trick play, you gotta know your options. I'm talking epidurals, natural birth, and C-sections—oh my!

First up: epidurals. Picture this: your partner is gritting her teeth, eyes narrowed, and says, "I need something for the pain." Enter the epidural, a medical Hail Mary that numbs the lower half of her body. Your role? Be the steady hand she needs. Sometimes, they'll ask her to curl up in a specific way so they can administer the medication properly. This is where you come in: provide a shoulder to lean on, both literally and metaphorically. And remember, the decision for pain relief is ultimately hers, so be her biggest fan either way.

Next: natural birth. If your partner opts to go all-natural, aka the "Bear Grylls of Childbirth," more power to her. This route avoids pain medications and often involves a variety of positions and natural coping techniques. You'll want to be well-versed in what these are, whether it's back massages, breathing exercises, or just doing your best impression of a motivational speaker. ("You can DO it!") Have a mental list of ways you can help her manage the pain—sometimes distraction is your best tool in the toolbox.

And now, C-sections. Sometimes, the game plan changes mid-way. Whether it's a planned decision or a last-minute audible, a C-Section is major surgery, and it comes with its own set of rules. You might be asked to suit up in full surgical attire. Trust me, you haven't lived until you've worn a hairnet and shoe covers. You'll be there primarily for emotional support; your job is to be the calm in her storm. You might even get the chance to peek over the curtain and see your baby being born. But remember, it's a sterile environment, so follow the rules and listen to the medical staff.

So there you go, the main paths your D-day might take. Each has its own challenges and opportunities for you to shine as the ultimate support person. No matter what, just remember the end goal is the same: a healthy baby and a healthy partner.

5.4 Medical Staff: Who's Who in the Delivery Room

What's cookin', future dad? Alright, so you've studied the playbook, you're suited up, and now you're stepping into the arena. But wait a minute, this place is crawling with people in scrubs! Who are they, and what's their game? Relax, chief, I've got you covered. Let's talk about the starting lineup in the delivery room so you know who's who when the clock starts ticking.

First off, the Obstetrician, or OB-GYN for short. This is the quarterback of the operation, the one calling the plays and making the big decisions. They'll be the one to catch your tiny human as they come into the world. Hopefully, this is a doc you and your partner have gotten to know over the past several months. You'll want to have full confidence in them, so don't be afraid to ask questions leading up to the day. Trust is key.

Next up, the Labor and Delivery Nurses. Think of them as the offensive line; they're the ones who will block and tackle for you and your partner throughout the whole shebang. They'll check vitals, administer medications, and guide you through the process. Seriously, these folks are angels in scrubs. Make friends, remember names, and, for the love of God, don't get in their way. They've got a job to do.

Oh, and let's not forget the Anesthesiologist, especially if an epidural or C-section is on the table. This person is like your special teams player, stepping onto the field for specific, crucial moments. When they show up, things are about to get real—or at least a lot more comfortable for your partner.

You might also encounter a Pediatrician or a Neonatologist. They're the referees who give your newborn the once-over to ensure everything's A-OK. Usually, they swoop in after the birth to check vital signs and reflexes and generally give your baby their first report card.

Some of you might be going a different route and have a Midwife or a Doula as part of your team. Think of a midwife as an alternative to an OB-GYN, especially if you're aiming for a more natural birth. A doula? She's like your personal coaching staff, there to support you both emotionally and physically, but not medically. They're awesome to have in your corner if that's your game plan.

Alright, last pro tip: No matter who's in the room, remember, you and your partner are the stars of this show. Everyone is there to support you in this Hall-of-Fame moment. So, feel free to ask questions, get clarifications, or ask for a timeout to discuss something with your partner.

5.6 The First Glimpse: Meeting Your Newborn

You've supported your partner like a champ and navigated the medical maze; now the moment is almost upon you. I'm talking about that first glimpse of your newborn. Trust me, this is the moment that redefines "game-changer."

So, let's set the stage. You're in the delivery room, the air is thick with anticipation, your partner's final push is about to happen, and then—voila! Your baby enters the world. Man, I wish there were words to describe that feeling, but nothing in the English language, or any language for that matter, can do it justice. It's as if every emotion you've ever felt gets packed into this single instant.

Now, what's the etiquette here? If you're up for it, and the medical team gives the thumbs-up, you might be able to cut the umbilical cord. Doing so is like the ceremonial "snip" that separates your little one from their nine-month life support. Don't worry, it's easier than it sounds, and the medical team will guide you. You're basically the guest of honor in a rite of passage that's as old as humanity itself.

The baby is usually quickly checked by the medical team, and assuming all is well, you'll likely have the chance for some immediate skin-to-skin contact. If not you, then definitely with Mom. This moment, known as the "Golden Hour," is more than just a Kodak opportunity. It's a crucial bonding time and helps the baby adjust to life outside the womb.

Here's where the tears usually kick in, big guy. It's okay, let 'em flow. Whether it's your partner, you, or even that burly nurse with the sleeve tattoos, there won't be a dry eye in the house. You might even laugh because, hey, emotions are weird, and this is a lot to take in.

Your baby might cry, too, and let me tell you, that first cry is the sweetest sound you'll ever hear. It's like life's way of announcing, "Hey, I've arrived, now deal with me!"

This first glimpse isn't just about what you see; it's about what you feel. In a split second, you go from being a guy mostly responsible for himself to a dad whose every thought includes this tiny, squirming bundle. Your priorities shift, your heart grows (figuratively, don't worry), and your sense of purpose multiplies. Alright, treasure this moment because it's one for the books.

5.7 Paperwork and Red Tape: What Needs to Be Done

Howdy, New Papa! If you're like me, by this point, you've been floating on Cloud Nine, awash in a mix of love, adrenaline, and probably a good amount of exhaustion. But before you drift too far into those heavenly daydreams, there's some earthbound stuff we need to address. Yep, it's the unsexy yet necessary topic of paperwork and red tape. Even in these magical moments, Uncle Sam wants his due diligence.

First up is the Birth Certificate. This is your kid's very first piece of official paper, like a rookie card, but for humans. The hospital will usually provide you with the forms, and they're pretty straightforward. You'll need to decide on a name if you haven't already—no pressure or anything—and you and your partner will need to sign off. Don't scribble or half-ass this one; it's a keepsake for the ages.

Social Security Card, anyone? You'll fill out another form for this bad boy right after the birth certificate. Again, the hospital will usually have these forms on hand. This number is your child's ticket to being a tax-paying citizen one day. Hey, we all have to start somewhere.

Now, let's talk insurance. You'll want to add your newest family member to your health insurance plan. The clock's ticking; you generally have about 30 days to get this done, or you might have to wait until the next enrollment period. Make a note or set a reminder; this one's a can't-miss.

Speaking of legalities, do you have a will? You should. Life just got real, and as the head honcho of this new family unit, you've got responsibilities. If you haven't set up a will or a trust, now's the time to consider it. We're talking guardianship, inheritance, the whole nine yards.

Alright, I know paperwork is about as exciting as watching paint dry, but this red tape is the ribbon that ties your new family package together. Once it's all sorted, you can return to the good stuff, like capturing those first precious moments on camera. Oh yeah, that's what's coming up next, so keep your eyes peeled!

5.8 Photos and Memories: Capturing the Moment

Hey there, Papa-Razzi! Fresh off the paperwork trail, you're probably eager to dive into something a bit more, well, heartwarming. So, let's talk about capturing those first epic moments with your newborn. I mean, let's be real: if it's not on Instagram, did it even happen? Just kidding. Sort of.

First things first: the Golden Rule. Always, and I mean ALWAYS, ask your partner before you start snapping away or posting anything. This isn't just a courtesy; it's like the law of the jungle for new dads. Your partner has just been through a physical and emotional gauntlet and might not be in the mood for a photo shoot. So, read the room.

Alright, got the green light? Great! Time to get those once-in-a-lifetime shots. You know, the ones that make everyone go "Awww" or get you those coveted "likes" from friends and family. But more importantly, the ones you'll look back on years from now, misty-eyed and nostalgic.

First up is the skin-to-skin contact photo. This moment, often within the first hour after birth, is emotional gold. The look on your partner's face, your face, and even that scrunched-up "What just happened?" look on your newborn's face—capture it.

Don't forget the details. I'm talking fingers and toes, folks. Tiny hands grasping your thumb, little feet that you'll swear doubled in size a month from now. These are the close-ups you'll want to remember.

Family portraits are also a must. Now, it might be just you, your partner, and the baby, but if you've got other family members around—like other kids or maybe a grandparent—get them in the frame. It's the first official photo of your expanded tribe, after all.

Oh, and here's a pro tip: Don't overlook the candid moments. You know, the unplanned, unposed, unaware shots. Maybe it's your partner gazing at the baby, the baby making a funny face, or even you caught mid-emotion. These are often the pics that end up being the most treasured.

And, hey, if you're not the best photographer, don't sweat it. Your skills lie in other areas, like mastering the art of diaper change or becoming a baby-burping black belt. But still, take those photos. You won't regret it.

Alright, the stage is set, the album's started, and you're feeling like a million bucks.

5.9 Recovery: The First 24 Hours

Hey, New Dad on the Block! Now that you've navigated the emotional whirlpool of birth, snapshots, and even tackled some red tape, you might be thinking it's time to kick back and relax. Hold onto your bootstraps, cowboy, because we've got one more frontier to explore: the first 24 hours of recovery.

Firstly, let me give you a pat on the back. You've done well, really well. But the real MVP is your partner, who's just done something akin to running a marathon while solving a Rubik's Cube. She's gonna be sore and tired, and her hormones will be tap-dancing like a Broadway show. Be ready to lend a hand, a shoulder, and maybe even an empathetic ear.

Your new mission, should you choose to accept it, is to become the Ultimate Support Guy. If Mom wants ice chips, you're on it. If she needs to adjust her position in bed but can't quite move, you're her personal pillow arranger. You get the gist; you're the Guy Friday to her Robinson Crusoe.

Let's talk food. After the birth, your partner might be ravenous, or she might not want to eat at all. Hospitals usually offer a post-birth meal, but let's be honest: hospital food is about as appealing as a root canal. If she's up for it, how about ordering her favorite meal? Just check with the medical staff to ensure she has no dietary restrictions.

Sleep—or the lack thereof—is also on the agenda. Look, you both are going to be tired, monumentally tired. But try to let her catch some Zs first. You can take the first shift of babywatching. Trust me, she's earned that nap more than anyone else in that hospital.

Now, about your bundle of joy. Babies have this cute trick where they sleep a lot in their first 24 hours. It's nature's way of giving parents a tiny break before the real fun begins. But when they're awake, they'll want to eat. Whether your partner is breastfeeding or you're using formula, these first feedings can be a bit tricky. Be there to help, offer encouragement, and maybe even hold the baby if she needs to adjust.

Last but not least, get ready for some visitors. Close family and friends will be eager to see the newborn and offer their congratulations. Coordinate with your partner about who gets the invite, and maybe set some boundaries for visiting hours. The last thing you want is a parade of people when you're both running on fumes.

Alright, champ. You've braved the birthing room and captured memories. You're officially not just a man but a dad—a title you'll wear for the rest of your life. Wear it with pride, and know you've got this today, tomorrow, and all the days to come.

CHAPTER 6:

The First Week: Welcome Home

6.1 Arrival: Setting the Stage at Home

Welcome to the fourth quarter, gents. You've navigated the labyrinth of pregnancy and survived the roller coaster of labor. Now, you're about to step into your home turf again. Only this time, you're not coming home as a couple; you're a full-fledged family. So, how do we ensure this homecoming is more of a smooth touchdown than a fumbled pass?

First up, let's talk safety. You might have lived in your house for years without incident, but kids have a sixth sense for finding hazards. Whether it's an exposed electrical socket or a cabinet full of cleaning supplies, you'll want to baby-proof that danger zone.

Let's talk about ground zero: the nursery. By now, you've probably got the crib, the changing table, and an armchair for those late-night feeding marathons. But have you anchored all this furniture to the wall? One good push from a curious toddler and that bookshelf could be a hazard. So grab a drill and some wall anchors, and make it happen.

Next: electrical outlets. These things are like magnets for tiny, curious fingers. Simple plastic outlet covers will do the trick. You pop them in, and voilà! No more electrically curious baby.

"But what about the kitchen?" I hear you ask. Excellent question. Little ones have a sixth sense for finding the one cabinet you forgot to lock. Go ahead and install those child safety locks. Yeah, they're annoying for adults, but you'll get used to the extra step when you realize it's saving your kiddo from a household disaster.

Now, let's talk trash, literally. Your garbage can is a treasure trove of "interesting" things for a baby. Get one with a locking lid, or simply place it in a locked cabinet. Sure, it's a small inconvenience for you, but the peace of mind is worth it.

Okay, you're nearly there, buddy. However, there's one more thing you might not have considered: the TV remote. It's usually loaded with small, shiny, and very swallowable batteries. A secure remote holder, or even a high shelf, can be a lifesaver.

Oh, and here's a pro tip: get on your hands and knees and crawl around. Seriously. Seeing your house from a baby's eye level reveals all sorts of interesting dangers you might have overlooked.

Even after all this, never underestimate the ingenuity of a toddler. Always keep an eye out and make adjustments as needed. Your little one is basically a mini MacGyver with a penchant for chaos.

That should get you started on your path to becoming the Safety Czar of your household. Baby-proofing isn't just about locking everything up; it's about creating an environment where your little explorer can learn and grow without turning your hair gray in the process.

Now, on to something often overlooked—the fridge. You've been eating hospital food or grabbing fast food for days, but once you're home, you'll want something more wholesome. Stock up on easy-to-cook or pre-made meals that you can heat in a jiffy. Trust me, neither of you will be in the mood for gourmet cooking the first week back.

Then there's the sleep situation. Ah, the elusive sleep. Your newborn is still working on understanding the concept of night and day, so prepare for some nocturnal adventures. Whether it's a comfortable rocking chair for those midnight feedings or a white noise machine to drown out city sounds, ensure you've got a sleep-friendly environment.

Create a changing station not just in the baby's room but also in your living area. Diaper changes come fast and frequently, and you don't want to be sprinting to the nursery every hour. A small basket with diapers, wipes, and other essentials can be a lifesaver.

And here's something you might not have thought of: set up a mini self-care station for you and your partner. I'm talking about a spot with some lotion, snacks, a water bottle, and perhaps even a book or magazine. During those quick breaks when the baby is napping, having a go-to place for a little recharge can do wonders.

So, those are the basics, my man. Bringing home a baby turns your everyday environment into a stage where a whole new act of your life will unfold. Ensure that stage is set to make your lives as hassle-free as possible.

6.2 Baby Gear: Operating Strollers, Car Seats, and Diapers

Gather 'round, dads, it's time for a crash course in Baby Gear 101. You may think you're a whiz with gadgets, but let me tell you, figuring out how to collapse a stroller with one hand while holding a crying baby in the other is the real ultimate skill test.

There are about a gazillion types on the market: jogging strollers, travel systems, double strollers—I could go on. The key here is to practice. And I mean really practice. Open it, close it, attach the car seat, detach it, and try steering it through your living room without knocking over a vase. If your stroller has a storage basket, figure out what you need easy access to when you're on the go. Diapers? Snacks? A flask of strong coffee? (Just kidding on that last one... mostly.)

Speaking of diapers, you've probably already done a few test runs at the hospital. But let me tell you, changing a diaper in the comfort of your home is a different ball game. The faster you get at this, the less chance you'll have of experiencing the dreaded "peeing mid-change" scenario.

But what about the other accessories, you ask? Baby monitors, bottle warmers, wipe warmers—oh my! Take it easy. A lot of these are nice-to-haves but not must-haves. Get the basics down first. Know how to warm a bottle in a bowl of warm water before you invest in a high-tech bottle warmer.

Now that we've covered the basics, you're better equipped to handle the arsenal of baby gear that's about to become a permanent fixture in your life. Trust me, mastering this early will make those first weeks at home much smoother. Up next, we're diving into the wacky world of baby sleep patterns. Get ready for a ride!

6.3 Sleep Deprivation: The New Normal

Well, my man, if you've always prided yourself on being an early riser, you're in luck. Because from here on out, you're not just rising early—you're practically never going to bed. Alright, I'm exaggerating, but not by much. Welcome to the zombie-like existence known as new parenthood. It's not just about sleepless nights; it's also about broken sleep, catnaps, and finding ways to function on fumes. So, let's talk strategies.

First off, if you've got the "I'll sleep when I'm dead" mentality, it's time for an overhaul. Lack of sleep is a torture technique for a reason. It messes with your judgment, reflexes, and general well-being. So, whenever someone offers the cliché "Sleep when the baby sleeps," don't roll your eyes. Take them up on it, even if it's just 20 minutes here and there. Your sanity will thank you.

Now, let's talk about the night shift. Consider dividing the night into shifts if you're bottle-feeding or mixing it up with breastfeeding. One of you takes the baby from, say, 9 PM to 2 AM, and the other takes over from 2 AM to morning. This way, both of you get at least one longer stretch of sleep. Trust me, in those early weeks, that's golden.

Remember, babies are not born with a circadian rhythm—that's something they develop over time. So, in the early days, expect your little one to be an unpredictable sleeper. You'll find all kinds of advice on establishing a sleep schedule, and while some of it may be useful down the line, for the first few weeks, you're pretty much in "anything goes" territory.

Caffeine will be tempting, and in moderation, it's a lifesaver. But beware—overdoing it can mess with your already fragile sleep and make you jittery, which is not a great combo when holding a fragile human. Stick to a cup or two a day and try not to consume it in the late afternoon or evening. You'll want to take advantage of any opportunity to rest, and a caffeine buzz can kill that chance.

This is also not the time to be a hero. If relatives or close friends offer to come over and watch the baby for a couple of hours while you catch some Zs, take them up on it. There's no award for doing it all on your own, and a couple of hours of uninterrupted sleep can feel like a week-long vacation at this stage.

In short, sleep deprivation is your new normal, but it's not a life sentence. As your baby grows, sleep will improve (for both of you), and this bleary-eyed chapter will become a distant memory. For now, grab sleep where you can, help each other out, and remember—you've got this.

6.4 Visitors: Managing the Crowds and Expectations

Ah, the moment your baby arrives, it's like the floodgates open. Everyone—grandparents, aunts, uncles, friends, neighbors, mail carriers (okay, maybe not them)—will be itching to get a glimpse of the newest member of your family. And while it's wonderful to be so loved, sometimes you just want to yell, "Give us a minute, would ya?!"

Let's tackle this diplomatically. First and foremost, set some ground rules. If you're the spontaneous type, this might sound like overkill, but believe me, a little planning goes a long way. Maybe you and your partner agree that immediate family can come to the hospital or home within the first few days, but everyone else should wait a week or two. Or maybe you're okay with a revolving door as long as people call first. Whatever it is, ensure you're both on the same page.

Oh, and by the way, having a "No Visitors" policy for a little while is perfectly acceptable. Some families prefer that cocooning period to adjust to their new life without the constant presence of guests. If that sounds like you, don't be shy about making that known. People will understand, and if they don't, that's their problem.

Now, let's talk about visitor etiquette. If someone's coming over, especially in those early days, it's absolutely okay to ask them to bring food or run a quick errand on the way. This isn't a social call; it's a support mission. They get the reward of baby cuddles, and you should get something, too, even if it's just a sandwich or a gallon of milk—fair's fair.

When visitors do arrive, be realistic about time limits. What I mean is, don't let anyone overstay their welcome. Your baby needs a feeding and nap routine (so do you, remember?), so it's totally fine to usher people out when it's time for the next feed or nap. A polite "Thanks for coming. It's about time for little Timmy's next feeding" is a gentle but clear signal that it's time to go.

Lastly, hygiene. From the time of COVID-19, this has taken on a whole new level of importance. It should go without saying that anyone feeling under the weather should stay far away from your newborn. Make hand sanitizer your new best friend, and don't be afraid to ask people to wash their hands before holding the baby. Your house, your rules.

Managing visitors can be a balancing act between showing off your beautiful new addition and maintaining some semblance of order in your newly chaotic life. A little planning, a lot of communication, and a dash of assertiveness will go a long way. Hang in there, champ, we're in this together.

6.5 The First Pediatrician Visit: What to Expect

So, you've managed to get through the first week or so with your newborn, you've mastered—or let's be real, at least attempted—the diaper change, and you've had your fill of visitors. Now, it's time to venture into the world for that first pediatrician visit. A tad nerve-wracking, isn't it? What do you bring? What will they ask? Will there be a quiz? Relax. This isn't your high school biology final. It's more like a get-to-know-you session where the only one being graded is probably the baby. So, let's break it down.

First things first, timing. Typically, the first pediatrician visit is within the first week after you bring the baby home. This is a brief examination to confirm that the baby is eating properly, putting on weight, and generally adapting to life outside the womb. The doctor will also want to ensure that jaundice, a common condition in newborns, isn't an issue.

Oh yeah, you'll have questions—everything from "Is this amount of spit-up normal?" to "How do you actually give a baby a bath without turning it into a splash zone?" Write them down because, trust me, sleep deprivation has a way of wiping your memory clean at the most inconvenient times.

The appointment itself is generally pretty straightforward. Expect lots of weighing, measuring, and a thorough once-over of your baby. They'll check reflexes, listen to the heart and lungs, and assess the soft spots on the baby's head known as fontanelles. It's all standard procedure, nothing to worry about.

Listen closely to what the pediatrician says. They'll give you guidelines about feeding, sleep patterns, and what developmental milestones to look for in the coming weeks. This is also your chance to ask those burning questions you've had since the baby arrived. No question is too small or too silly. These folks have heard it all.

Oh, and here's a pro tip: Use your phone to record the important points of the conversation. It's a lot to take in, especially on Team No Sleep, and it's super helpful to have something to refer back to later.

The first pediatrician visit is a rite of passage for new parents. Sure, you'll probably leave with more questions than you had going in, but that's okay. That's what the pediatrician is there for—to guide you through this maze called parenthood.

6.6 Feeding: Breast, Formula, and Sleepless Nights

Ah, feeding—the beautiful, sometimes maddening cornerstone of newborn life. If you think about it, food is pretty much your little one's entire world right now—that and sleep. But let's focus on the edible side of things. Whether your partner is breastfeeding or you're going the formula route, there's a lot for you to wrap your head around. Grab your bottle opener—no, not for that kind of bottle—and let's dig in.

First up, breastfeeding. If your partner is breastfeeding, you might feel a bit like a fifth wheel. What's your role, right? Well, buddy, you're the pit crew in this Formula 1 race. Be there with water, snacks, and emotional support. Breastfeeding can be a marathon, and every marathoner needs their hydration and energy replenished.

Now, formula feeding. If you're going this route, you're in the driver's seat a bit more. Learn how to prepare a bottle correctly and safely. You'd think mixing water and powder would be straightforward, but you'd be surprised at how many nuances there are. Ensure you follow the instructions on the formula package to a T. Too much water, and your kid isn't getting the nutrients they need. Too little, and you could risk dehydration. And let's not forget, always check the bottle's temperature before giving it to your baby.

Then comes the actual feeding. Whether it's breast or bottle, that baby's gonna eat roughly every 2-3 hours in the beginning, day and night. Yep, you read that right. It's an around-the-clock gig. Even if you're not the one actually feeding the baby, you can still be a huge help. Offer to take the late-night or early-morning feeding if you're using formula, or be the one to get up and bring the baby to Mom for breastfeeding. Every little bit helps.

And there you have it, your quick guide to feeding your new bundle of joy. It's a steep learning curve, but it's a curve everyone who's ever had a baby has had to navigate. You'll get the hang of it; if you don't, well, there's always takeout. Up next, we'll talk about the epic adventures of diapering. Get ready; this is where it gets really dirty. But hey, you've got this, man!

6.7 Hygiene for Two: Bath Time and Diapers

Welcome to the splash zone, my man! Bath time and diapers aren't just necessities; they're bonding opportunities. And both of you get to be naked and vulnerable, so there's that leveler. Alright, enough small talk.

Grab your rubber ducky and a towel. It's time to dive into the wondrous world of baby hygiene.

Let's start with bath time. Baby tubs are great; however, a kitchen sink can do the trick in a pinch. But wait, don't fill that tub just yet. Babies don't need to be bathed daily. In reality, frequent bathing can lead to dry skin for babies. A couple of times a week is sufficient unless, of course, a poop-splosion or some other mess that requires immediate action. Always test the water with your elbow to ensure it's not too hot or too cold. Babies are like Goldilocks; they like it just right.

So, you've got your water temperature perfect. Now what? Gentle baby soap, a soft washcloth, and your hands are all you really need. No loofahs, no harsh soaps, and absolutely no adult shampoo; we're keeping it simple here. Oh, and keep one hand on your baby at all times. Those little wrigglers can slide faster than you can say "Baby on board."

Alright, now let's talk diapers. You will become a master at this, like it or not. There's no secret handshake for the Diaper Changing Club, but there is a technique: lift the baby's legs, slide a fresh diaper under, wipe, remove the old diaper, and seal up the new one, all while avoiding any sudden streams of you-know-what (boys, I'm looking at you). Easy, right? Practice makes perfect, or at least less messy.

Wipes are your Swiss Army knife in this arena. They're good for butts, hands, faces, and sometimes even cleaning a spill in a pinch. Keep 'em handy everywhere: diaper bag, car, living room, even your man cave. You never know when you'll need one.

Diaper rash? It's like the baby version of an athlete's foot. Get yourself some diaper cream and apply liberally. And give the little tush some air once in a while. Skin likes to breathe, even the tiny baby kind.

Quick word on diaper disposal: you might be tempted to get one of those fancy, twist-and-seal contraptions that promise to lock away odors for eternity. To be honest, a standard garbage bin with a cover does the job well, as long as you're consistent about taking out the trash. Plus, you save on those overpriced proprietary bag refills. Money better spent on coffee, if you ask me.

And there you have it, gentlemen. You are now officially ready for bath time and diaper duty. It might sound daunting, but it's one of those things that becomes second nature before you know it. You'll be a pro and have some great stories for when your kid brings home their first date. But let's not get ahead of ourselves.

6.8 Mom's Recovery: How to Be Supportive

Listen up, gents. While doing your touchdown dance after successfully navigating diapers and baby baths, remember that the woman who just brought your mini-me into the world is going through her fourth-quarter recovery. And believe me, it's not just about shedding pregnancy weight or getting back into pre-baby jeans. We're talking physical healing, hormonal roller coasters, and let's not forget, she's probably as sleep-deprived as you are—maybe more. Here's how you can be the MVP in this game.

Firstly, let's talk about wounds of war—stitches, C-section scars, or just general soreness. Your partner is healing. This isn't the time for her to lift anything heavier than your newborn or do anything more strenuous than breastfeeding or bottle feeding. So, roll up those sleeves and become the household chore champion you never knew you could be. Dishes, laundry, vacuuming—you've got this, man.

Next, let's discuss the elephant in the room: hormones. Her body just went from being a baby-making factory to a milk-producing one, all in the span of, well, a moment. Hormones are resetting, and this can affect mood. It's not the time for debates, arguments, or unsolicited advice. Be there, be supportive, listen. If she wants to cry at a cereal commercial, hand her the tissues and tell her it really is a moving piece of cinematography.

Mealtime is crucial. She needs fuel, especially if she's breastfeeding. The best thing you can do? Make sure there are easy-to-grab snacks and meals at hand. And no, a bag of chips doesn't cut it. Think protein bars, fruit, pre-made smoothies, and sandwiches. You're basically running room service for a few weeks, so embrace your inner bellhop.

Speaking of breastfeeding, it's not as easy as it looks. There can be issues—latching problems, milk supply concerns, and sometimes, downright frustration. Your role? Be the cheerleader, not the coach. If she opts for formula, that's fine, too. Fed is best, and it's really none of anyone else's business how your baby gets their nutrition.

Ah, sleep—or the lack thereof. Here's where you can really shine. Take turns with the baby so she can get a few solid hours of uninterrupted sleep. Yes, you'll be tired too, but hey, that's why they invented coffee, right? This is a team sport, after all.

Lastly, keep an eye out for signs of postpartum depression. If she seems excessively down or anxious for a prolonged period, encourage her to talk to a medical professional. You can't fix it, but you can absolutely be there to offer your unwavering support.

The playbook on supporting Mom's recovery. It's not glamorous, but it's necessary and will earn you more points than you can imagine.

6.9 Postpartum: Navigating Emotional Waters

So, you've successfully crossed the finish line. The baby's here, Mom's recovering, and you're probably up to your elbows in diapers and baby wipes. Pat yourself on the back, my friend; you've done well. But hold the champagne—there's another leg to this marathon that many don't talk about: the emotional postpartum journey.

For starters, yes, you're exhausted. You're on Team No Sleep, and that in itself is a recipe for emotions running high. If you find yourself snapping over spilled milk—literally—take a deep breath and remember, it's not just you feeling the weight of this new world order. Your partner is right there in the trenches with you, and she's been through a bodily ordeal to boot.

Moms often experience something called "Mom Guilt." It's like buyer's remorse but for parenting decisions. Be the voice of reason if she's beating herself up for taking a longer shower while you watch the baby or fretting over formula feeding instead of breastfeeding. Tell her she's doing a great job because, let's be real, she is.

Next, help her carve out "Me Time," even if it's just a half-hour where she can read, take a bath, or binge a couple of episodes of a show she likes. A little time to herself can recharge her batteries and make a world of difference for both her and, by extension, you.

Don't forget about "We Time" too. That's right, date nights aren't a relic of the past. They just look a little different now. It could be a home-cooked dinner after the baby's asleep or a movie night with popcorn. It doesn't have to be fancy; it just has to be time spent together as adults, not just co-parents.

Alright, here's one for the men out there. It's okay for you to have feelings about this whole dad gig, too. There's a term for it—Dad Guilt. Yeah, it's a thing. Maybe you're back at work and feel like you're missing out, or perhaps you feel like you're not doing enough around the house. Share these feelings with your partner; you're in this together.

To sum it up, navigating the emotional waters postpartum is like sailing: you have to read the winds, adjust your sails, and sometimes weather the storm together. The good news? The storms do pass, and when they do, you find yourself in clearer, calmer waters.

6.10 Teamwork: Sharing the Load Fairly

Alright, buddy, pop quiz: what's the most crucial ingredient in keeping your relationship solid while transitioning into parenthood? If you answered "teamwork," give yourself a pat on the back—or better yet, change the next diaper as your reward.

Parenting, my friend, is not a solo sport. It's a tag team match where communication and fair play are your best strategies. Now, by 'fair,' I don't mean splitting every duty down the middle 50/50. Trust me, sometimes one of you will shoulder more of the load, and that's okay. What's crucial is that both of you feel the distribution is equitable, given your individual capacities and external commitments.

First things first, let's talk about nightly duties. You know the drill: baby cries, baby needs a diaper change, baby wants to eat, rinse and repeat. Tailor it to your schedules, but make sure you're both getting some sleep. I promise it makes a world of difference to your mood and patience levels.

Then comes housework. Yep, with a newborn, your home turns into a whirlpool of onesies, baby bottles, and toys quicker than you can say "diaper rash." The key here is not to wait for her to ask for help. Be proactive. Do the dishes, vacuum the living room, or take out the trash. And if you notice the laundry hamper's full, don't walk past it like it's invisible. Tackle it head-on; it's just another opponent in this tag team match.

How about time off? Both of you need breaks; don't forget that. Take turns going out for a coffee or a jog. An hour or two of alone time can feel like a mini-vacation when you're deep in the trenches of new parenthood.

And hey, about baby care—don't let her monopolize it because she's "better at it" or "knows what she's doing." You need to get in the game to learn the ropes. So, change diapers, rock the baby to sleep, or give them a bottle or a bath. Being involved doesn't make you less of a man; it makes you more of a dad.

Lastly, be each other's cheerleaders. Celebrate the small victories, whether it's finally getting the baby to latch on for feeding or managing to assemble the high chair without any leftover pieces. A simple "You're doing great" can go a long way.

CHAPTER 7:

Weeks Two to Four: Finding Your Rhythm

7.1 Establishing Routines: Setting Up for Long-term Success

Welcome to Chapter 7, my man. By now, you're officially navigating the post-birth waters, and hopefully, the ship hasn't sunk yet. Now, you might think that with a newborn, the concept of "routine" is as fictional as a unicorn playing a ukulele. But let me tell you, establishing some sort of daily cadence is not just possible; it's vital—for your sanity and the baby's.

First, don't get too fixated on the word "routine." We're not talking military precision here, just a general framework to structure your day around. Newborns are the very definition of unpredictability, so flexibility is your friend. But even a loose routine can offer a sense of normality when your world seems like it's been flipped upside down.

Start with the basics. Feeding time and nap time are pillars around which you can start building your day. You'll notice that the little one will naturally start to settle into some sort of cycle (after a chaotic few weeks, mind you). As tempting as it might be to let them sleep whenever and wherever, try sticking to the "crib for naps, arms for cuddles" rule. Consistency is key.

But what about your routine? Yes, you, the guy who used to wake up at noon on weekends and consider a breakfast burrito a culinary achievement. Let's be real: those days are behind you, at least for now. New dads often underestimate how much their own routine impacts their baby's. So, set your alarm, grab a shower, and have some breakfast—even if it's a few spoonfuls of oatmeal while rocking a fussy baby. Trust me, feeling somewhat human can give you the energy to tackle the day ahead.

If you're back at work, use your mornings wisely. Pack your work bag the night before, prep some easy breakfasts for the week, and have your work clothes ready to go. In the evenings, your new wind-down routine might involve less Netflix and more swaddling, but that's okay. Prioritize sharing some meaningful moments with your partner after the baby is asleep for the evening, even if that simply entails enjoying each other's company in peaceful quietude on the sofa.

Weekends are no longer just for leisure; they're prime time for planning. Use this time to stock up on essentials, run errands, and maybe even meal prep for the week. Also, weekends are a good opportunity for longer outings with the baby, which can serve as dry runs for potential pitfalls like diaper disasters or public meltdowns.

Lastly, keep a small notebook or use an app to jot down some notes about how things are going, especially in the beginning. Are certain feeding times causing fussiness? Is the baby napping better in a darker room? Tracking these little details can help you tweak your routine for better efficiency and, ultimately, happier days for everyone involved.

Alright, that's enough about routines. Trust me, you'll get the hang of it, and before you know it, you'll be a pro at juggling dad duties with everything else.

7.2 Handling Stress: When Both of You are on Edge

Let's talk about something as unavoidable as dirty diapers—stress. It's not just you; everyone in the household is feeling it. But let me tell you, if you handle stress like you're diffusing a ticking time bomb, you're setting yourself up for more explosions down the road. So, let's roll up those sleeves and get into the nitty-gritty of stress management.

First off, let's establish something: it's okay to feel stressed. You're dealing with a tiny, shrieking human who seems to have an insatiable hunger and a knack for crying just when you've closed your eyes. If you didn't feel stressed, I'd recommend checking your pulse. However, it's the way you handle stress that makes all the difference.

You remember those good ol' days when stress meant deciding whether to watch another episode or call it a night? Those were cute times. Nowadays, stress is more about figuring out why your child won't stop crying or how you'll manage to function on three hours of sleep. But you can still learn a lot from how you used to manage stress.

Let's begin with the fundamentals—inhaling deeply. I get that it seems overly simplistic, yet even a couple of profound breaths can significantly reduce your tension. Do it with me—inhale deeply through your nose, hold it for a few seconds, and exhale fully through your mouth. Ah, feel that? That's your nervous system taking a chill pill.

Now, what about the stress that comes from disagreements between you and your partner? Remember, you're both sailing in the same stormy waters and snapping at each other is as helpful as a hole in your lifeboat. When tempers flare, the best thing to do is to step away, even if it's just into the next room, and cool off. Return to the issue when you've both got your sea legs back. A bit of perspective can turn mountains into molehills.

And look, I get it. When you're stressed, exercise might be the last thing on your mind. But a quick jog around the block or even a 10-minute workout at home can work wonders for your stress levels. You don't have to become a fitness guru; just get that blood pumping and those endorphins flowing.

Lastly, don't underestimate the power of a good laugh. Whether watching a funny video clip or recounting a hilarious mishap that happened during the day, laughter really is the best medicine. Even better, it's contagious. A little humor can go a long way in easing tension and reminding you that, despite the challenges, there's joy to be found in this new chapter of life.

Alright, I've armed you with some solid stress-busting strategies. Use them wisely, and remember, you're not in this alone.

7.3 Communication: Keeping the Lines Open

Ready for the next round of dad-vice? We've chatted about handling stress, so let's pivot to something that could make or break any relationship, especially during these newborn days—communication. And no, I'm not talking about texting each other from different rooms in the house. I mean the real deal, the face-to-face "How the heck are we doing?" kinda talk.

You see, communication is like oil to a machine; without it, things get rusty and stop working smoothly. However, if you think you've been communicating all this while, the baby will throw a wrench in your gearbox. Your partner's not a mind reader, and neither are you, even though it would make life a whole lot easier if you were.

First off, let's debunk a myth: talking more doesn't necessarily mean better communication. It's not about the volume, fellas. It's about the quality. In between changing diapers and late-night feedings, find a few quiet moments to ask your partner how she's feeling, physically and emotionally. These aren't trick questions; they're bridges to better understanding.

Speaking of emotions, let's get real. You're going to have a ton of them—some you can easily identify and others that make zero sense. Don't bottle them up. Share what you're feeling, too. Remember, vulnerability isn't weakness; it's the cornerstone of a strong partnership.

Active listening is another crucial element. When your partner talks, really hear what she's saying. Put down that phone, make eye contact, and listen. Give feedback where needed, and if it's your turn to spill the beans, don't hold back. A relationship is a two-way street, after all.

Oh, and keep an eye out for non-verbal cues. Your partner might not always say when she's exhausted or needs help, but her body language will scream it from the rooftops. If you notice her shoulders slumping or she's sighing more than usual, take the hint. Step up your game, offer to take over some chores or baby duties, and give her some much-needed rest.

And now, for the elephant in the room: disagreements. They're going to happen, buddy, and that's okay. But how you handle them can set the tone for your relationship moving forward. No shouting matches, alright? No one wins those. Keep calm, state your point of view, and aim for compromise, not victory.

Let's say you both disagree about something like baby sleep training methods. Instead of digging your heels in, try to find a middle ground. Maybe you can agree to try one method for a week and see how it goes, then regroup and discuss any tweaks or changes. The key is to make decisions together, like the co-captains of the good ship Family.

In summary, keep those lines of communication open and oiled. Remember, you and your partner are navigating this new world together. No one's an expert out of the gate, but with clear and open communication, you're more likely to enjoy the journey.

7.4 Health Checks: Keeping Up with Doctor Appointments

Time to talk about a topic that's as exciting as watching paint dry but way more crucial—doctor appointments. I get it; keeping track of dates and times while juggling a newborn, sleep deprivation, and possibly a full-time job sounds about as fun as stepping on a LEGO brick. But this stuff's important, so let's dive in.

First things first: the baby isn't the only one who needs to see a doc. Sure, pediatrician visits are frequent and vital for tracking growth, immunizations, and all that jazz. But what about you and your partner? After childbirth, your partner will have some postpartum checkups to attend, and it's not just a "walk in, walk out" deal. These appointments are vital for her well-being, covering everything from physical recovery to emotional health.

So, here's the deal: go with her. Yep, you heard me. It's not just moral support; it's about being engaged. Plus, it's a chance to ask questions and clarify doubts. Many of us guys think the doctor's office is a mysterious temple where we dare not tread. Nah, man, get in there!

As for your own health, don't neglect it. I know it sounds counterintuitive when there's so much going on, but you've got to be in top shape to be the dad you want to be. If you've been putting off a check-up, now's the time to get back on track.

Keep a calendar—a physical one hanging in your kitchen or a shared digital one—to jot down all the upcoming appointments. This will also help you see the big picture, spotting any potential scheduling conflicts well in advance. Trust me; the last thing you want is to realize you've double-booked yourself when you're already running on fumes.

And don't forget the impromptu visits. Sometimes, you'll have to make an unplanned trip to the doctor because of a fever, rash, or some unidentifiable baby goo. Life happens. Always have an emergency bag packed with necessities such as diapers, baby wipes, and an extra outfit for those unexpected doctor visits.

Listen, I get that doctor appointments can be nerve-wracking, especially when it involves your newborn. But think of it this way: each visit is a checkpoint, a small reassurance that you're doing alright in this marathon called parenthood.

So, lads, keep those calendars up to date, those go-bags packed, and those questions ready for your doctor. Your family's health is a team effort, and you're a key player.

7.5 Baby Milestones: What to Look For

Time to talk about something that'll bring out your inner spectator and turn you into a full-time cheerleader—baby milestones. This isn't the Olympics, but watching your little one roll over for the first time might as well be a gold-medal event in your household.

So what are these milestones, and why do they get everyone so jazzed up? Essentially, milestones are markers of your baby's development. They're the building blocks of growth, both physically and mentally. We're talking about the first smile, first crawl, first steps, and those adorable first words. But hold your horses—before you start daydreaming about baby's first Harvard acceptance letter, let's ground ourselves in the here and now.

One of the first milestones you'll probably notice is the social smile. That's when your little one smiles back at you, and you realize they're not just a food-consuming, diaper-filling machine. This usually happens around the 6- to 8-week mark. If you're not in the room when it happens for the first time, you'll swear on your life that the dog, the cat, or a particularly fascinating spot on the wall stole your big moment. That's why you've got to keep those eyes peeled, man!

Following the first smile are other "firsts": first laugh, first word, and first steps.

Now, each baby is different, and there's a wide range of what's considered "normal." You might have a friend whose kid walked at nine months and feel like your 12-month-old is slacking because they're still crawling. Cool your jets! Babies develop at their own pace, and comparing them to others is like comparing apples to—well, other kinds of apples that just ripen at different times.

On the flip side, if you're worried that your child is missing milestones or there are consistent delays, don't go down the rabbit hole of late-night Google searches. Talk to your pediatrician. That's what they're there for, and they can provide context and advice based on actual medical knowledge. Radical idea, right?

Teething is another significant event that usually kicks in around six months but can start as early as three months. It's a painful process for both the baby and, by extension, you. However, teething rings, cold washcloths, and appropriate medication can provide some relief.

Introducing solid foods is a fun but challenging milestone that usually occurs around six months. It's a messy affair but a crucial step in your child's nutritional development. As always, consult with your pediatrician for advice tailored to your child's needs. Initial foods are often single-ingredient and not likely to cause allergies, like rice cereal, but each baby is different.

Your baby's cognitive and motor skills will also develop rapidly during this time. You'll soon notice them trying to grab things, recognizing familiar faces, and maybe even saying "Mama" or "Dada" (and, believe it or not, it's usually "Dada" that comes first!).

Between the ages of one and two, you'll start to see more of your child's personality emerge. They'll begin to explore the world around them more independently (yes, this means baby-proofing the house), and they'll start to develop likes and dislikes, particularly when it comes to food and toys.

Potty training is another milestone many parents dread, usually occurring between 18 months and three years. There's no one-size-fits-all advice here; patience, encouragement, and maybe a few rewards (stickers work wonders) will be your best friends during this challenging time.

A pro tip: keep a journal or use one of those baby milestone apps. Documenting these moments isn't just for show-and-tell or social media bragging rights; it's a useful record for tracking development. You can share this info with the doc and have it as a keepsake for years to come.

Just a heads up, you'll soon discover that milestones aren't just about the baby. They're emotional landmarks for you, too. The first time your baby grips your finger or laughs at your goofy faces, you'll feel like the king of the world.

So, buddy, break out the camera and get ready to cheer. Your little one's on a developmental marathon, and you've got front-row seats.

7.6 Out and About: When to Take Baby Outside

Alright, my adventurous padawans, who's getting cabin fever? I bet you're itching to venture beyond the four walls of your home, the diaper station, and that incessantly looping lullaby playlist. If you're wondering when it's okay to take your little astronaut out into the great, wide world, this one's for you.

First off, let's bust a myth: no, you don't have to wait for an arbitrary number of months before exposing your kid to the glory of fresh air and sunshine. Babies are not like paintings that need to be kept out of natural light to preserve their value. However, you do have to exercise some common sense.

For the first couple of weeks, you might want to keep it low-key—your backyard, a brief walk around the block, that sort of thing. The big reason is that your baby's immune system is still booting up. While it's doing its Windows 95 impression, you'll want to minimize exposure to germy situations.

Don't forget to check the weather. You want your baby's first outdoor experience to be pleasant, not a test of their resilience against a polar vortex or a Sahara heatwave. Babies can't regulate their body temperature as well as we rugged adults, so overdressing or underdressing them can cause problems. Rule of thumb: dress them in one more layer than you'd wear yourself.

Now, what about the grand tour? The mall, the supermarket, the (holy of holies) hardware store? Wait until you and your co-pilot—your partner—feel comfortable. Every family's comfort level will differ. Some might be ready for a Target run by week three; others may prefer to wait a bit longer. Listen to your gut, and consult the boss (your partner, obviously).

When you decide to hit the town, keep your trips short and sweet, especially at the beginning. Remember, the world is like an IMAX theater for your baby. The lights are brighter, the sounds are louder, and the number of new smells is off the charts. It's thrilling but also can be overwhelming.

Safety's a big deal, too. If you're driving, ensure the car seat is installed correctly. The hospital probably checked it when you first took your newborn home, but it doesn't hurt to double-check. And no, the baby doesn't go in the front seat. I know, buddy, it's a bummer not to have your wingman riding shotgun, but safety first!

So, gear up, gentlemen. Your first outing might not be an epic quest worthy of tales sung by minstrels, but it's the start of many adventures you'll have as a family. And like any good adventure, it'll have its bumps and surprises. That's what makes it memorable.

7.7 Work-life Balance: Returning to the Job

Gentlemen, let's chat about the office battlefield, shall we?

First things first: ditch the guilt. I know, it's easier said than done. You might feel like you're abandoning your partner and your tiny squire in the middle of a crucial quest. But here's the truth: you've got a role to play outside of the home too, my friend. The best thing you can do for your family is to provide for them, which often means returning to work. Just remember, your family also needs you emotionally and physically present, so keep that in balance.

Ah, the art of delegation. If you have a set of tasks that need to be accomplished at home, don't play hero and try to do them all yourself. Sure, you're Captain Fantastic and all that, but even superheroes have sidekicks. Assign some duties to family members or close friends who offer to help. Grandparents often jump at the chance to be involved, which can free you up to handle other things.

Emails, meetings, deadlines—they'll all be there waiting, but here's the kicker: they don't have the same adorable smile that'll greet you when you walk through the door at the end of the day. Make the most of your time at work so you can make the most of your time at home.

7.8 Date Night: Rekindling the Flame

Ah, date night. Remember those? A table for two, candlelight, and conversations that didn't involve diaper sizes or baby formula brands. It may seem like those days are buried under an avalanche of onesies and pacifiers, but I assure you, they're not extinct—they're just hibernating.

Let's break down how to resurrect the ancient art of dating your spouse, even in these wild times. Don't worry; you don't have to pull a James Bond to rekindle the spark. Sometimes, a superhero's most powerful weapon is his calendar. Yeah, you heard me. If you can schedule meetings and doctor appointments, you can schedule romance. Pick a day, any day, and carve out some time for just the two of you.

"But what about the baby?" I hear you ask. Fair point, rookie. This is where your village comes in. Grandparents, friends who owe you a favor, trustworthy babysitters—these folks can be your MVPs for the evening. Just ensure you've briefed the caregiver about feeding schedules, bedtime rituals, and where to find the baby's favorite stuffed animal.

Now, onto the date itself. Listen, you don't have to break the bank to woo your partner. Sometimes, a simple dinner is all it takes to remind both of you that you're not just co-CEOs of a start-up called "Our Family." You're partners, lovers, and friends. Choose a spot that brings back good memories, or try a new place you both have been itching to explore.

Alright, the big night's here, and you're out the door. Turn off "dad mode" for a bit; I promise the world will keep turning. Avoid talking about baby stuff too much. This night is about reconnecting with each other, not strategizing the next diaper change.

What's that? You can't help but check your phone for updates? Look, it's natural to worry but trust your babysitter. Every five-minute text check is another moment you're not present with your partner. So, put the phone down. No, really, put it down.

At the end of the night, as you drive back home (maybe a little slower than usual, not ready for the night to end), take a moment to reminisce. You're still the same dynamic duo, even if there's a new addition to your team.

And guess what? The baby's fine, and you've had a blast and earned some much-needed adult conversation and eye contact. The mission, should you choose to accept it, is to not let another millennium pass before the next date night. You're fighting the good fight, buddy, and it's essential to remember who you're fighting alongside.

7.9 Solo Parenting: Handling Baby Alone

So, the moment has come. You're home alone with the little one, and your partner has stepped out—maybe it's back to work, maybe it's a well-deserved day out with friends, or perhaps it's just a grocery run. But here you are, just you and the baby, and maybe a family pet looking bewildered by the new dynamics. Welcome to Solo Parenting 101.

Before you break into a cold sweat, let me reassure you: you've got this. It might sound like a pep talk from a sports movie, but sometimes clichés exist for a reason. Trust your instincts; they're more reliable than you think.

First things first: preparation. If you're a gamer, think of this as setting up your save points. The diaper station? Check. Bottles or formula? Check. An assortment of toys to prevent meltdowns? Double-check. Knowing where everything is will give you that extra confidence boost.

Now, let's talk strategy. When you're on your own, juggling becomes your new best friend. Feeding, napping, playing, and the occasional poop-splosion (oh, they will happen)—it's like spinning plates, and it's your show for now. So, embrace the chaos.

What about the unexpected? "The baby won't stop crying!" you say.

Rule number one: stay calm. Babies are like Jedi masters at sensing your emotional state. Take a deep breath and systematically go through the checklist. Diaper? Hunger? Need to burp? Overtired? Once you've identified the issue, half the battle's won.

Don't underestimate the power of a good distraction, either. Got a playlist that your little one enjoys? Hit play. A walk around the block usually does wonders. It's all about your toolkit of distractions; deploy as needed.

But hey, you're not a robot programmed to fulfill baby needs. Take moments for yourself when the baby is content or napping. Sipping some coffee, quickly scanning the latest sports updates, or merely enjoying a quiet moment gazing out the window are your ways to press the "reset" button.

And remember, it's okay to ask for help. If you're genuinely overwhelmed, a quick call to your partner or a family member can provide real-time solutions or at least a momentary break from the solo gig.

As you wave goodbye when your partner returns, you'll realize something: you did it. You solo-parented like a pro. The baby's happy, you're still standing, and you've gained XP points in the Dad Game. And who knows? Maybe next time, you'll be the one teaching other dads how to rock the solo parenting world.

7.10 The Baby Book: Documenting the First Month

So, you've survived the first few weeks of fatherhood. Your sleep schedule is in shambles, your diet probably consists of whatever's quickest to make or order, and you've gotten to a point where the scent of baby wipes is your new cologne. In the blur of it all, let's not forget something pretty important—the memories. Welcome to the art of baby bookkeeping, or as I like to call it, "Not letting the good stuff slip away."

Now, you're probably thinking, "A baby book? Isn't that old school? We have smartphones for that." True, you could snap a hundred photos a day, but let's be real: those photos often end up lost in the digital abyss, forgotten until your phone helpfully reminds you years later.

So, let's start simple. Get yourself a good old-fashioned journal or a baby-specific book with spaces for notes and pictures. Trust me, in a world of chaos, a dedicated space to jot down milestones or stick a memorable photo can be priceless.

First, document the basics: the first time your baby smiled, the first coo, or the first time they gripped your finger. Each "first" is like hitting a mini-jackpot in the parenting casino, and you will want to remember these.

Next, we get to the funny, quirky stuff. Did your baby make a hilarious face the first time they tasted something new? Did they discover their feet and can't stop playing with them? These are the lighter moments that break up the routine, and they're golden. Jot them down.

"But what if I forget?" you ask. That's where tech comes in. Whenever something noteworthy happens, make a quick note on your phone. Then, once a week, transfer those notes to your baby book. Think of it as updating your operating system but in a more analog way.

Photos! Don't just stick to the "official" milestone pics; throw in some candids and some "real-life" snaps. You, bleary-eyed but happy; your partner, holding the baby like a pro; even that pile of dirty diapers as a testament to your new role as the Diaper King. They all tell a story, your story.

Lastly, remember this isn't just for you or the baby when they're older. It's also for your partner. While handling the role of a documentarian, don't forget to note how your partner is doing—first time Mom had a full night's sleep, the first time she went out post-baby, etc.

Years down the line, when you're flipping through this book, it will be a time machine. You'll remember the good, the tough, and the downright silly, and you'll be glad you took a few minutes here and there to capture it all.

Alright, my man. You're up-to-speed on documenting the first month. Your legacy as a super-dad is taking shape.

CHAPTER 8:

The Final Stretch: Completing the First Month

8.1 The One-month Checkup: Charting Growth and Development

If you've reached this chapter, congrats! You're one month into this parenting gig. It's almost time for a little victory dance, but not just yet. This milestone comes with a mission: the one-month checkup. No, it's not some exotic cocktail or a trendy restaurant; it's your baby's first real, in-depth health screening. And it's vital.

Firstly, understand that this is more than just a weigh-in. Sure, they'll check the weight, height, and circumference of your baby's noggin, but it goes beyond that. Physicians will search for indicators that your infant is on track in terms of both physical and emotional growth. They'll assess motor skills, responses to stimuli, and even emotional connection. It's a full MOT for your tiny human and crucial data for peace of mind and future planning.

The doc will probably fire off a series of questions at you. "Is the baby eating well?" "How's sleep going?" "Any concerns?" These aren't casual ice-breakers; they're diagnostic tools. Your answers will help the doc assess if everything is progressing as it should. So, be honest. This isn't the time to downplay or exaggerate. Your doctor is your ally, not a judgy in-law.

You might be asked to hold your baby in certain positions during the exam. It's a bit like playing a low-stakes game of Twister. Left hand on green! Right foot on blue! Except in this game, green and blue are "Check for hip alignment" and "Test the Moro reflex." And yes, you'll learn what a Moro reflex is; consider it a rite of passage.

Expect vaccinations, too. Brace yourself because watching your baby get poked with needles can be tougher on you than on them. But remember, these jabs are like force fields against diseases you don't want anywhere near your kid.

Before you leave, you'll probably get a printout charting your baby's stats. It's like a baseball card but for new humans. Some parents stick these on the fridge, a testament to surviving the first month.

All in all, the one-month checkup is your first official pit stop in this Formula 1 race called parenthood. You'll refuel on information, get some new tires in the form of vaccines, and get the all-clear to keep racing down this exhilarating, exhausting, amazing track.

8.2 Sex After Baby: When and How to Reconnect

Look, I get it. The last thing you've probably had time to think about amid the sleepless nights and non-stop diaper changes is getting frisky. But let's be honest here; intimacy is a big part of a healthy relationship, and sooner or later, you will be wondering how to get back into the groove.

Now, don't go marching into the bedroom with a "business as usual" attitude. Your partner's body has been through the Olympics of physical feats, and she's got a whole lot of healing and adjusting to do. First things first: Wait for the green light from the doc. Usually, the standard wait time is around six weeks postpartum, but every body is different. Listen to what the medical pros say; they know their stuff.

Once you get the all-clear, start slow. And I mean snail-pace slow. This isn't the time for your best James Bond impression; it's more like a Mr. Rogers' "Let's be considerate and gentle" episode. Foreplay isn't just a pre-game warm-up now; it's the main event. Emotionally reconnect before you dive into the physical. A simple touch, a long hug, or even a meaningful look can reignite the sparks that made fireworks in the first place.

And let's chat logistics. You've got a new roommate now, and this one has ears like a hawk and the lungs of an opera singer. Timing is everything. Coordinate with the baby's naptime or enlist one of your trusty support network members for babysitting duty. Whatever you do, ensure you won't be interrupted by cries from the next room. Nothing kills the mood faster than a wailing baby—trust me on that.

The venue may need to change too. Maybe the bedroom is now more of a war zone with baby gear strewn all around. Consider other locations in your home where you can find a semblance of privacy and romantic ambiance—even if that means a clean couch in the living room.

Let's also address the elephant in the room: exhaustion. You're both running on fumes most days. That's okay. Intimacy doesn't always have to lead to the full monty. Sometimes, a passionate kiss or a loving cuddle is enough to keep the flame alive. You're in this for the long haul, remember? There'll be time for more as life starts to settle down.

So, there you go. Take it slow, be considerate, and adapt. This is yet another chapter in your evolving relationship, and like everything else you've faced so far, you'll get through it together.

8.3 Post-baby Fitness: Getting Back in Shape

So, you've been eating for two, huh? I get it. Those midnight ice cream runs for your partner weren't exactly kind to your waistline, and let's not even talk about the takeout binges. The dad bod might be in fashion for some, but if you're itching to get back to your pre-baby physique—or at least close to it—then listen up.

First, you might think a new gym membership is the ticket. Hold on there, Rocky. Remember, time is a commodity you're running short on these days. There's a crying, eating, pooping time-sink at home that requires your attention. So, let's be real: hitting the gym for an hour a day might not be in the cards.

Instead, think about workouts that can be squeezed into your day-to-day life. Ever tried doing lunges while bottle-feeding? How about bicep curls with a diaper bag? You laugh, but hey, desperate times call for desperate measures. The point is to use what you have. Ten minutes here and there can add up.

The basics are always good, man. Push-ups, sit-ups, lunges, and squats. These can be done at home, and best of all, they require zero equipment. Aim to get at least 150 minutes of moderate exercise per week, as the pros recommend, but feel free to break that down into bite-sized chunks that fit your schedule.

If you're more of a "get out and go" type, consider taking the baby for a brisk walk in the stroller. Not only will this get you moving, but it's also a great way for the little one to take in some fresh air and sights. Plus, it gives your partner a well-deserved break. It's a win-win.

Don't overlook your diet, either. I know it's easy just to grab a slice of pizza or a fast-food burger between baby duties, but that won't help you or your energy levels. Simple home-cooked meals with lean proteins, whole grains, and lots of veggies will make a world of difference. Think of it as fuel for your newly hectic life.

Lastly, rope in your partner for some couples' workouts if you can. It's a good bonding experience and creates a sense of teamwork. Additionally, some friendly rivalry is beneficial for everyone.

Getting back in shape post-baby isn't just about looking good; it's about feeling good and being healthy for your family. Remember, you've got a little one looking up to you now—be the superhero they think you are.

8.4 Family Traditions: Starting New Ones or Continuing Old Ones

Ah, traditions. Every family's got 'em. Whether it's the ritual of Sunday dinners or the yearly trek to some remote cabin in the woods, traditions are the glue that holds families together. Now that you've added a new member to the tribe, you're probably wondering: Do we stick with the old ways, or is it time to shake things up?

First, no law says you can't keep doing what you've always done. If Grandma's Thanksgiving dinner is the highlight of your year, by all means, keep the tradition alive. But don't be afraid to tweak things a bit to accommodate the new, tiny human in your life. Your family will get it—everyone's been through this before.

However, the arrival of your little one is also a perfect excuse to start some new traditions. How about a weekly "Family Game Night" where even the baby gets to roll some dice? Alright, maybe they're not ready for board games yet, but you can still lay them on a blanket in the middle of the action. Or consider a yearly "New Place" visit where you explore somewhere none of you have ever been. This could even be as simple as a different park or a zoo.

You might also want to introduce some rituals that are especially for the baby. Reading a bedtime story every night, for example, isn't just good for their brain development but also establishes a comforting routine. These early traditions can be particularly meaningful and offer a sense of stability for your child as they grow.

Now, let's talk about the holidays. Yeah, you might have celebrated Christmas or Hanukkah or whatever your flavor of winter festivity is in a certain way for decades, but adding a child into the mix means rethinking how you do things. Maybe your all-night New Year's Eve parties are a thing of the past, but you can still ring in the new year with a more kid-friendly event—like a "Noon Year's Eve" party where the ball drops at midday.

The key to traditions, old or new, is that they offer a sense of continuity and stability. In a world that's always changing—especially your world, now filled with diapers, late-night feedings, and a constant sense of exhaustion—having something to look forward to can be reassuring for everyone involved.

So go ahead and make new traditions or stick with the old ones. Just ensure to involve the newest member of your family. After all, they're the reason you're reading this book, right?

8.5 Guilt and Doubt: How to Deal with New Parent Emotions

One useful way to combat both guilt and doubt is through open communication with your partner. Chances are they're going through the same emotional whirlwind. Talking openly about your feelings can help both of you realize that you're not alone. Often, just vocalizing these emotions can lessen their grip on you.

Doubt is guilt's sneaky cousin. It creeps in when you feel vulnerable and makes you question your choices. "Is the baby really okay? Am I doing enough? What if I mess this up?" Doubt can be paralyzing, but here's the thing—everyone makes mistakes. You'll put the diaper on backward at least once and might even forget a feeding time. It's okay. Children are remarkably resilient and don't expect you to be perfect; they just need you to love them and be there for them.

Another tool in your emotional arsenal should be self-compassion. Cut yourself some slack; you're navigating an entirely new phase of life. You wouldn't berate a friend for making a small mistake, so why do it to yourself? Being a new parent is tough, and it's essential to acknowledge that. Give yourself permission to take a break or even to fail occasionally.

You can also seek external support. Whether it's a support group for new parents, a trustworthy pediatrician, or just a group of friends who've been there, don't underestimate the value of a strong support network. Sometimes, the best way to dispel doubt and alleviate guilt is to hear from others who've walked the path before you.

Remember, you're in this for the long haul, and you'll have countless opportunities to get it right—or wrong. Either way, each experience is a lesson, not a life sentence. Guilt and doubt will occasionally visit, but they don't have to move in and live with you.

8.6 Celebrating One Month: Reflecting on the Journey

Congratulations, you've made it through the first month of parenthood! This milestone is not just an achievement for you but for your entire family. As you've juggled sleepless nights, endless diapers, and the whirlwind of emotions, you've also navigated the complexities of relationships, work, and self-care. This chapter is dedicated to pausing and taking stock of your journey because while the first month may be over, the path ahead is long, and reflection is a crucial tool in your parenting arsenal.

Begin by recognizing your achievements, no matter how small. Did you manage to get a few hours of uninterrupted sleep? That's a win. These small victories can act like stepping stones, leading you toward a deeper understanding of your new role as a parent.

Next, think about the challenges you've faced. It's not just about congratulating yourself on the wins; it's also about understanding where you struggled. Did you feel overwhelmed by your new responsibilities? Did you and your partner have disagreements about childcare roles? Being honest about these challenges doesn't make you a bad parent; it makes you a reflective one, willing to grow and adapt.

Discuss these reflections with your partner. A shared journey is made easier when both of you are on the same page. Talk openly about your experiences, fears, and hopes for the future.

This one-month mark is also an excellent opportunity to reassess your support systems. How are your friends and family contributing to your new life? Do you need to set boundaries or ask for specific types of help? Relationships outside your immediate family are crucial but should also be conducive to your new lifestyle.

Finally, set goals for the next month. Whether it's getting the baby on a sleep schedule, planning a date night, or starting to think about going back to work, having objectives gives you something to work toward. But remember, these goals should be flexible. Parenting is unpredictable, and it's okay to adjust your expectations as you go along.

So, as you celebrate this one-month milestone, take a moment to breathe, reflect, and prepare. The journey of parenthood is a marathon, not a sprint, and you've just crossed one of many milestones on this incredible path.

CHAPTER 9:

Beyond the First Month: What Comes Next

9.1 The New Normal: Accepting Your Changed Life

If there's one constant in the life of a new parent, it's change. Your old routines have been thrown out the window, replaced by a new, unpredictable schedule governed by a tiny human's needs. Welcome to your new normal. This chapter aims to help you embrace the profound alterations to your lifestyle, making room for growth, learning, and lots of love.

First things first: let go of your old expectations. Parenting textbooks and your well-meaning aunt might have given you a list of what to expect when you're expecting, but the real thing is a different beast altogether. Your baby hasn't read those books and doesn't care for schedules or societal norms. They have their rhythm, and part of your job is to get in sync.

It's time to redefine what productivity means to you. Pre-baby, a productive day might have involved meeting work deadlines, hitting the gym, and cooking a three-course meal. Now, if you've managed to shower, catch a few hours of sleep, and keep your baby fed and happy, you're doing exceptionally well. Celebrate the wins, no matter how small they may seem in comparison to your previous life.

Your social circle will change, and that's okay. Some friendships might drift, others will strengthen, and you'll forge new relationships with fellow parents. The dynamics are different, and it's a good idea to surround yourself with people who understand what you're going through. Don't see this as a loss but as a natural evolution of your social life.

As for your relationship with your partner, intimacy takes on a new form. With the exhaustion and demands of parenthood, you may find that candle-lit dinners and spontaneous weekend getaways are things of the past—at least for now. Emotional support, shared laughter over a baby's cute antics, or a simple hug at the end of a long day can be just as intimate and rewarding.

Financially, be prepared for a shift in priorities. Your money is not just yours anymore; it's a resource for your family. Budgeting takes on a new level of importance. Whether saving for education or buying diapers, you'll need to plan more than you did before.

Adjusting to your new normal doesn't happen overnight. It's a gradual process that requires patience, resilience, and a good sense of humor. Embrace the journey with open arms, and don't forget to pause and cherish the simple moments. These are the building blocks of your new life.

9.2 Vaccinations and Health: Keeping Baby Protected

Welcome to another essential chapter in your journey as a new dad—immunizations and overall well-being for your newborn. The landscape of healthcare may feel like a labyrinth of decisions and responsibilities but don't worry. This chapter will guide you through the essential milestones and choices that lie ahead.

First and foremost, let's talk about vaccinations. These are non-negotiables in the modern world. Not only do they protect your child from potentially fatal diseases, but they also contribute to the health of the community at large. Many vaccinations need to be administered in a specific sequence, often beginning in the first few months of life, so it's crucial to consult with your pediatrician and stick to the schedule.

Though anti-vaccine movements have gained some traction on social media, the scientific consensus supports vaccinations as safe and crucial for public health. Talk to your doctor, read reputable sources, and make an informed decision. Misinformation can be detrimental to your child's health, so make sure you're consulting credible experts.

Apart from vaccines, regular check-ups are key to tracking your baby's development and catching any potential health issues early on.

Nutrition is another cornerstone of your child's well-being. Whether you and your partner have opted for breastfeeding, formula, or a combination of both, ensure you follow the best practices and guidelines for your chosen method. Nutritional needs will also evolve as your baby grows, so stay in the loop with your pediatrician to adjust as necessary.

Hygiene, believe it or not, is not just about those endless diaper changes. Learn how to trim those tiny nails and maintain oral care (even before teeth come in). A clean baby is generally a happy baby, and good hygiene can prevent several health issues down the line.

Finally, mental health starts early. While your newborn won't be experiencing stress like adults, providing a calm and stable environment is critical for their psychological well-being. Hold them, talk to them, play soothing music, and engage in simple play activities that stimulate their senses but don't overstimulate. You are your baby's first experience with the world; make it as positive as possible.

Immunizations and ongoing healthcare may seem like just another task on your ever-growing checklist, but they are crucial for your child's long-term health. And remember, you're not alone. Healthcare providers, your partner, and your support network are all part of the team.

9.3 Grandparents: Managing the New Family Dynamics

Ah, grandparents—the doting figures who bring another layer of love, spoiling, and, yes, sometimes unsolicited advice into the parenting equation. As you navigate this new chapter of your life, it's essential to think about managing relationships with grandparents effectively, particularly as they are likely eager to be a part of your baby's life. In this chapter, let's explore how to create a harmonious balance that benefits everyone.

One of the biggest joys of having a child is seeing your own parents transform into grandparents. They might shower the baby with gifts, offer to babysit, and share stories of raising you when you were a baby. These can be heartwarming moments, but setting boundaries from the get-go is important.

If the grandparents are overly excited and you find their enthusiasm overwhelming, have an open and honest conversation with them. Explain your parenting style and what you're comfortable with regarding their involvement. Remember, tact is key here, as emotions can run high.

Perhaps you've decided to follow a particular parenting philosophy, like attachment parenting or a strict feeding schedule. It's essential to communicate this to the grandparents so that they can respect your wishes when they're spending time with the baby. It's not about telling them they were wrong in how they raised you; it's about them understanding how you are choosing to raise your child.

Grandparents often come with a wealth of parenting experience, and their advice, sometimes unsolicited, can be invaluable. However, parenting norms change. Practices deemed safe or appropriate a generation ago might not be recommended today. Keeping grandparents informed with current guidelines is crucial, particularly when it concerns your child's well-being and safety. Consider sharing books or articles that align with your parenting style or even inviting them to a pediatrician's appointment to hear the advice firsthand.

One common issue is the "spoiling" factor. Grandparents love to spoil their grandchildren, which is generally fine in moderation. However, if it starts interfering with your child's routine or behavior, it's time for a discussion. For instance, if bedtime becomes a battle after a day with grandparents who don't enforce your rules, kindly reiterate the importance of keeping a consistent routine.

Last but not least, the emotional support that grandparents can offer is priceless. Allow them to build a special relationship with your child. This bond benefits your baby and gives you time to catch a break or even go on a much-needed date night.

In sum, grandparents can be a fantastic resource and support system, but like any relationship, it requires work, communication, and mutual respect. As you find your footing in these new family dynamics, keep the lines of communication open and work together for the sake of the newest family member.

9.4 Childcare: Considering Your Options

Now, it's time to tackle another significant issue: childcare. Selecting the right childcare is paramount as you and your partner return to work or simply need a few hours to yourselves. In this chapter, we're diving into the world of nannies, daycare centers, and family support to help you decide what's best for your family.

One of the first things to consider is your budget. Childcare is often one of the most significant expenses for new parents, and prices can vary wildly depending on your location and choice of childcare. Daycare centers, for example, often offer the most structured environment but can be more expensive than hiring a nanny. On the other hand, while a nanny can offer more personalized care and flexibility, costs can add up, particularly if you're considering a live-in option.

Once you've determined what's financially feasible, consider your child's needs and your own expectations. Would your child benefit more from the social interaction and structured activities that a daycare center provides? Or are you looking for more personalized attention and the comfort of your home? Addressing these considerations will steer you toward the most suitable option.

In the information age, it's easier than ever to research potential childcare options, but that can also make the process overwhelming. Begin by asking for advice from loved ones or friends, or consult online parenting communities. Personal experience from people you trust can give you invaluable insights you won't find in a brochure.

Visiting potential childcare options is crucial. Whether it's a daycare or a family member who's offered to help, spend some time observing. You'll get a sense of the environment, the caregivers, and how other children are treated. Take note of staff-to-child ratios, cleanliness, safety measures, and the overall vibe. Don't hesitate to ask questions; this is where your child may spend a significant amount of time, after all.

Don't forget about the "gut feeling" factor. Sometimes, a place can look great on paper but might not feel right. Trust your instincts.

Also, consider backup options. There will be days when your nanny calls in sick or your daycare center closes for a holiday. Having a plan B (and even a plan C) can save you a lot of stress in the long run.

Last but not least, communicate with your partner throughout this process. Both of you should be comfortable with the choice, as you'll both be interacting with the childcare provider and dealing with any issues.

Choosing the right childcare option is a complex decision that involves a myriad of factors, from cost to emotional comfort. As you weigh your options, take your time, research, and trust your parental instincts. The right choice will set the stage for your child's well-being and give you peace of mind as you navigate the waters of new parenthood.

9.10 The End Book: A Conclusion Based on All Chapters

As we draw the curtain on this extensive journey through pregnancy and early parenthood, it's time for some reflection. We've navigated the highs and lows, the sleepless nights, and those miraculous mornings when your little one greets you with a smile that melts away all the exhaustion. But remember, while this book may be reaching its conclusion, your journey is just beginning.

From the thrill of that initial positive pregnancy test to the whirlwind of feelings and duties that ensue, we've delved into a wide array of subjects. We've examined everything from pregnancy symptoms and health, the minefield of cravings, and the importance of maintaining intimacy and teamwork with your partner to the practicalities of labor, feeding, and baby-proofing your home. The aim was to provide a comprehensive guide that you can always refer back to, no matter what stage of the journey you find yourself in.

However, if there's one central message to take away from all of this, it's that every parent's journey is unique. While guides and how-tos can be helpful, your instincts and your partner's will be your most trusted allies. Parenthood isn't a one-size-fits-all hat; it's a custom-tailored experience you and your family create together.

Let's also acknowledge that perfection is a myth. Mistakes are a part of the learning process, and it's okay not to know everything right off the bat. Whether it's spilling formula everywhere on your first go or accidentally snapping a photo of your thumb during your baby's first smile, errors are the stepping stones to mastery and, more importantly, to some fantastic stories to embarrass your child with when they're older.

It's important to maintain a sense of humor throughout this journey. Parenting is perhaps the only job where you can go from being peed on to experiencing pure, unconditional love within the span of a few minutes. It's a wild ride that's best met with a good dose of laughter and a lot of patience.

Finally, remember that you're not alone. Lean on your support network, keep the communication lines open with your partner, and don't hesitate to ask for help. Whether you're a stay-at-home parent or juggling a career, whether you've planned every detail or are winging it—this experience is yours to shape, and an entire community of parents out there is in it with you.

Thank you for letting this book be a part of your incredible journey into parenthood. May it serve as a helpful companion, a source of comfort, and a toolkit full of tips and tricks that make your life just a tad bit easier. Here's to many more ups than downs, laughter than tears, and endless love as you and your family grow.

The end? Hardly. It's just the beginning. Welcome to the incredible world of being someone's dad. You've got this!

Printed in Great Britain
by Amazon .

39937606R00066